Traces of the Trinity

Traces of the Trinity

Signs, Sacraments and Sharing God's Life

Andrew Robinson

Ⓒ

James Clarke & Co

James Clarke & Co
P.O. Box 60
Cambridge
CB1 2NT
United Kingdom

www.jamesclarke.co
publishing@jamesclarke.co

ISBN: 978 0 227 17443 2

British Library Cataloguing in Publication Data
A record is available from the British Library

Contents

Part I
The Trinity and the Structure of Signs

Part II
Sharing God's Life

Part III
The Mystery of Existence

Figures

*For my friends who, like me, are wondering about their place
in the church and about the church's place in the world.*

Acknowledgements

My many intellectual debts have been largely acknowledged in my more academic publications. Here I especially thank Philip Clayton, Nicola Hoggard Creegan, F. LeRon Shults, Christopher Southgate and Kenneth Wilson for helping me at a crucial juncture to think about what I wanted to do in this book. Charles Hewlings, Kevin Hooke, Sarah Horsman, Peter Hurst, Philip Law, Tirke Linnemann, Terry Nottage, Jane Robinson, Jo Robinson, Chris Southgate, Stephen Tomlin, and my friends at the *Agape* group in Newton Abbot, jointly held me to the task of making clarity my priority. Adrian Brink, Fiona Christie, Bethany Churchard and Emily Reacher at James Clarke & Co. have been notably helpful and efficient in steering the book through the publication process. I thank Matthew Tomlin for constructing the diagrams and Lawrence Osborn for proofreading the text.

The work on which this book draws benefited greatly from a series of grants from the STARS (Science and Transcendence Advanced Research Series) programme of the Center for Theology and the Natural Sciences in Berkeley, California, supported by the John Templeton Foundation. I am also grateful to the Ian Ramsey Centre for Science and Religion at the University of Oxford and to the Centre for Naturalism and Christian Semantics at the University of Copenhagen, whose respective invitations near the beginning and end of the writing process gave me opportunities to test this way of presenting things.

Key Terms and Biblical Quotations

A glossary of key terms is provided at the end of the book. Biblical quotations are from the New Revised Standard Version unless otherwise indicated.

Preface

The 'doctrine' of the Trinity ought to be more than just a theory about God, if it is a 'theory' at all. Rather, trinitarian thought should be a framework that makes sense of the entirety of Christian life. It should change the way we understand God's ways with the world, make a difference to how we live our lives, condition the way we see things, and provide a context for all our decisions and actions. If we are honest though, it is questionable whether the life of the church would look very much different if trinitarian ways of speaking about God were to be quietly dropped. Affirmation of God as Trinity is supposed to be the touchstone of Christian orthodoxy. But for most people the idea of God as Trinity seems abstract, remote and irrelevant.

The aim of this book is to make a contribution towards rectifying this strange situation. To that end, I will be inviting you to look at Christian theology through a new lens. The lens I offer to put into your hands is fashioned from the theory of signs; that is, from philosophical insights about the nature of representation and interpretation. Technically, the study of signs is called semiotics, from the Greek word *semeion,* a sign. The field of semiotics is notorious for being rather difficult and obscure, which, at first sight, might be considered a barrier to making it the basis of a user-friendly instrument for theological exploration. However, the underlying principles of the theory of signs are rather simple and beautiful. Part of my task will be to invite you to see this beauty as reflecting something of the eternal being of God.

There is nothing inherently new or unorthodox about a semiotic approach to Christian theology. For example, St Augustine's writings on the interpretation of Scripture, on the sacraments, and on God as Trinity, are all shaped by a theory of signs. This fits, of course, with a belief that, "In the beginning was the *Word,"* and that Jesus is the *"image* of the invisible God." Not that I am claiming quite the level of originality of Augustine and his like. Part of Augustine's achievement was to have developed his theory of signs for himself. I, in contrast, will be making use of ideas about the nature of representation and interpretation that I have learned elsewhere: largely from the work of the American philosopher–scientist Charles S. Peirce (1839-1914).

For reasons that are not entirely accidental, Peirce's theory of signs (and, by the way, his name is pronounced 'purse') has deep resonances with Augustine's. Unlike Augustine, however, Peirce's own writings are not easy reading for the non-specialist. My reasons for having spent the best part of two decades wrestling with the implications of Peirce's thought need not be elaborated here. Suffice it to say that my book, *God and the World of Signs* (Leiden: Brill, 2010), was an attempt to draw on Peirce's semiotics as a framework for developing Christian theology in a way that takes current scientific insights, especially those of evolutionary biology, with utmost seriousness.

It had always been my intention to follow *God and the World of Signs* with something more accessible. Two things particularly influenced the way I proceeded . The first was that the distinguished philosopher of religion, Keith Ward, wrote a review of the book in which he lamented the fact that I had stuck so closely to Peirce's formulations. "In the end," he wrote, "while it is fascinating to learn about Peirce, I think Robinson's account stands on its own, and that if he could devise a vocabulary less opaque than Peirce's this would be of great benefit to scholarly discussion."[1]

After feeling some initial annoyance at this criticism – after all, it had been precisely my aim to show how Peirce's brilliant but difficult thought might be of use to theology – I came to see that Ward was probably right. Now was the time to try to set out my scheme as a whole without risking the reader becoming stranded in a Peircean quagmire. I resolved, therefore, to try to present a theology shaped by Peirce's theory of signs without mentioning (or at least rarely mentioning) Peirce. Where his terminology seems opaque or otherwise unhelpful I have been unapologetic in changing it, and I have avoided continual references to Peirce's writings or to the secondary literature.

Those unfamiliar with Peirce may ask themselves where the boundary lies between Peirce's philosophy and my own appropriation of it for theological purposes. Broadly speaking, anything I say about the structure of signs derives from Peirce, while the theological applications of Peirce's semiotics are my own. (What

1 *Reviews in Science and Religion*, May 2011, pp. 31-34.

Peirce himself thought about theology in general and the Trinity in particular is another matter, which other scholars have tackled.) My overall intention is that the book should be accessible to the general reader, as well as interesting to more specialized theologians. I hope that neither will be offended to find that my tone is, in places, decidedly non-academic.

The second thing that helped crystallize the shape of the book was that I began to turn my thoughts to attempting a semiotic account of the sacraments. Part of my reason for not having done so sooner was, paradoxically, that the sacraments were one of the few areas of theological inquiry to have already been touched by various kinds of semiotic thinking over the centuries. I knew, therefore, that some careful thought was going to have to go into the question of what my semiotic approach might have to offer. What I hadn't anticipated was quite how personally challenging it would be when my attempts to think through the sacraments met up with questions that were increasingly troubling me about the church – what is it, where is it, and what is my place in it? Writing this book therefore became part of my way of trying to answer those questions for myself.

The result is an attempt at a theological synthesis based upon three original proposals. The first is a 'semiotic model' of the Trinity – a way of thinking about God as Trinity using current philosophical ideas about the nature of representation and interpretation. The second is an attempt to develop this approach as a way of thinking about what it might mean to talk about our 'participation' in God's own life. The third, which ties in with the first two, is a way of seeing the world as bearing traces – vestiges, as the tradition has sometimes called them – of the triune being of God.

I hope that, for non-specialist readers, the book will be engaging enough to make trinitarian theology relevant to their everyday lives and experience. I also hope that readers at the more academic end of the spectrum will be prepared to tolerate the relatively non-academic style of the book for the sake of gaining a rapid sense of what is original – as well as essentially orthodox – about the synthesis. In spite of the deliberate sparsity of scholarly references, these readers should have no difficulty in working out whether they think this way of seeing things holds any promise.

Part I

The Trinity and the Structure of Signs

1

"You See a Cloud Rising"

On a gantry over the M5 motorway outside Exeter, there is a large electronic sign that normally displays information about traffic conditions, road works and so on. For a little while the sign has been showing the message, "Sign not in use." I always chuckle to myself when I see this. For of course the sign *is* in use: it is being used to convey the message that it is not in use.

When I tell people I'm interested in signs I am often met with rather puzzled looks. What do I mean by 'signs'? What is there to say about them? That most people haven't heard of the academic field of semiotics – the philosophical study of signs and signification – doesn't particularly surprise or upset me. What is interesting about those blank looks is that they reflect the fact that we are normally almost entirely unaware of our immersion in a world of signs, and equally unaware of our continual and habitual interpretations of those signs.

In truth, we live and move and have our being in a sea of signs – some of them made deliberately for the purpose of signifying, others simply aspects of the natural world that are capable of providing information. Within this medium of 'signification' we are like fish in water, completely dependent on our capacity to navigate the world of signs but mostly unaware of the medium itself. Indeed, if we were fully conscious of our constant interpretations of our surroundings we would come to a standstill. Just as our internal bodily functions work best if left to the unconscious parts of our nervous system, so most of our navigation of the world of signs is best done subconsciously. This is why a road sign can be programmed with the message "sign not in use" without much risk that the general driving population will worry about such a self-referential contradiction. In fact, the very need to display this message is itself a reflection of our propensity automatically to seek out meanings in things. Presumably, the concern of the Highways Agency is that if the sign is left blank its very blankness will be open to misinterpretation – taken, for example, as a sign that there are no major hazards ahead when perhaps there may be.

So, we interpret signs without thinking, as we must if we are not to become paralysed by unnecessary internal semiotic analysis. Signs are ever-present but almost completely invisible to us at a conscious level; for our self-preservation and sanity, our minds have evolved that way. One of the tasks of Part I of this book will be to enable you to bring some aspects of signs and their interpretations to the forefront of your awareness. This is not so that you can permanently reverse the transparency of signs: that would be impractical and possibly dangerous. Rather, it is so that every now and again you might choose to notice something of the structure of representation and interpretation. My thesis is that by foregrounding the nature of signs, we encounter the most fundamental aspects of being and thereby meet with the reality and closeness of God.

In order to show how that may be so, we will begin by examining the different kinds of relationship between signs and the things they signify. As the book progresses, we will find that signification has many dimensions. When we consider these further dimensions of signification, we will see that certain underlying patterns emerge. My suggestion is that these underlying patterns are related in some way to the 'three-ness' of God's inner being.

Why, though, would it be of any interest to find some sort of parallel between the structure of signs and the ways in which Christian theologians have found themselves compelled to speak about God? In other words, what could be gained by seeking a new way of articulating a trinitarian understanding of how God relates to the world?

The short answer to this lies in the recognition of a paradox at the heart of Christian belief. The paradox is this: affirmation of God as Trinity is supposed to be the touchstone of Christian orthodoxy, yet it is difficult to see that belief in the Trinity really makes much difference to the everyday thoughts and lives of ordinary Christians. As the twentieth-century German theologian Karl Rahner once put it: "despite their orthodox confession of the Trinity, Christians are, in their practical life, almost mere 'monotheists'." The same passage continues: "We must be willing to admit that, should the doctrine of the Trinity have to be dropped as false, the major part of religious literature could well remain virtually unchanged."[1]

Of course, I would be a fool to suggest that things have not moved on since Rahner wrote that in 1967. In the last few decades there has been a genuine revival of interest in the Trinity, at least within academic Christian thought. However, I venture to suggest that things have not changed as much as some would like to suppose.

1 Karl Rahner, *The Trinity* (New York: Crossroad Herder, 1999, first published in German 1967), pp. 10-11.

New books on the Trinity are continually appearing and many Christian theologians go to great lengths to assert their trinitarian credentials. But note that in the passage quoted above Rahner refers to the *practical* life of Christians, and I have my doubts about how much effect the resurgence of academic interest in the Trinity has had on ordinary Christian understanding and practice.

I know that some contemporary defenders of the relevance of trinitarian thought would immediately disagree with me, pointing out that the great insight of trinitarian theology is that all being is 'relational', and that a recognition of the inherent relationality of existence has enormous potential to influence the way we live our lives. Understanding God as persons-in-relation gives us a moral imperative to resist selfish individualism and build better communities. While I welcome this ethical impulse, I fear that seeing it as the main conclusion to be drawn from trinitarian thought amounts to a domestication of the Trinity, leaving the really radical implications of the doctrine untouched. It's not that I think that all talk of trinitarian relationality is misguided. Rather, I think that in its common forms it risks short-changing us. If there is something important in the doctrine of the Trinity, then it must be more than a rather general lesson about the relational basis of reality, a lesson that we could certainly have learned in other ways. And if we just want to invoke the Trinity to vindicate a perspective that we wish to adopt anyway, then aren't we getting things rather the wrong way round? There must, surely, be more to trinitarian thought than this.

The key to understanding what this 'more' might be lies, I want to suggest, in the structure of signs.

❀

Luke tells us that a growing crowd had been so enthusiastic to hear Jesus speak they had been climbing over one another to get to the front. Those who managed to get near enough would have heard the following somewhat exasperated observation:

> When you see a cloud rising in the west, you immediately say, "It is going to rain"; and so it happens. And when you see the south wind blowing, you say, "There will be scorching heat"; and it happens. You hypocrites! You know how to interpret the appearance of earth and sky, but why do you not know how to interpret the present time? (Luke 12: 54-56)[2]

---

2 In the similar saying in Matthew 16: 2-3, Jesus refers to "signs of the times."

The obvious and perfectly proper question we might ask ourselves about this passage is: What did Jesus mean by interpreting the signs of the present time, and what inferences did he wish his hearers to draw about the relation of the present to the future? I ask you, though, to set aside that question for the moment, and instead consider some more mundane questions about signs in general: What is a sign, and what different kinds of sign are there? What is happening when we interpret the appearance of a cloud as a sign that rain is on the way, or the direction of the wind as a predictor of how warm the weather will be?

In Jesus' illustration the cloud is a sign of (it can be taken to stand for, represent or signify) impending rain. The simplest answer to the question, "what is a sign?" is: a sign is *something that stands for something else*. The question of what exactly is required for something to be able to signify something else will be the subject of our investigations in this chapter and the next. For the moment, it is enough to say that when I use the term 'representation', I am referring to something that stands for, or that signifies, something. When I use the word 'signification', I am referring in a fairly vague way to what is going on when a sign is taken to represent something other than itself.

I suggested at the beginning of the chapter that we are not normally aware of the fact that we make our way in the world by continually interpreting the various kinds of sign around us. One of the curious effects of this transparency of signs is that we don't usually stop to reflect on how peculiar it is that anything should ever stand for something else. Why would we want to take something to represent something different? Another question that might occur after realizing the importance of signs in our lives is: Does the world have to have any particular 'structure' for it to be possible for things to have meanings or significance, for something to be taken as something other than what it is? We may begin to find some clues if we think through the various ways in which something can stand for something else.

In what way does a cloud rising in the west signify the likelihood of rain, or a wind blowing from the south give rise to an expectation of a scorching heat? We might say that the kinds of sign Jesus is referring to here are 'natural' signs. The signs he uses to illustrate his point are aspects of the natural world that we have learned to interpret in order to make predictions about the weather. If we see clouds we can predict rain; if the wind turns southerly we can (in some parts of the world) predict warmer weather. And our predictions based on these signs are reasonably reliable. As Jesus says, "and it happens."

Why is it that clouds and wind can act as fairly reliable signs of what sort of weather to expect? The answer is that there is an actual causal connection between the sign (clouds) and the thing the sign is taken to stand for (imminent rain). The clouds contain the moisture that may fall as rain, so the presence of clouds (rather than clear blue sky) increases the chance that it is going to rain.

The American philosopher–scientist Charles Peirce devised an elaborate set of terms to describe various aspects of the structure of signs. Many of his terms are notoriously obscure, but an aspect of his terminology that has become quite established is his distinction between three kinds of way in which a sign can stand for an object. Peirce labelled these three kinds of 'sign–object relation' indexes, icons and symbols. We will come to icons and symbols shortly. The kind of sign involved when we interpret the appearance of the sky as a predictor of the weather is an index. An index is a sign that is related to its object by some direct connection. Clouds are a sign of rain because rain (the 'object') comes from clouds (the 'sign'). There is a direct causal link between clouds and rain, so that even if it is not raining at the moment we may take the presence of clouds as a sign (index) of an increased chance of rain.

In my work as a medical doctor, I am continually interpreting indexical signs. The signs and symptoms of disease are indexes. A certain kind of rash is a sign of chicken-pox because the chicken-pox virus has a particular kind of effect on the skin. A certain kind of pattern on an electrocardiogram is a sign that a heart attack has occurred, because damage to heart muscle has a particular kind of effect on the conduction of electrical impulses through the heart.

It is no coincidence that the founders of the field of semiotics were the Ancient Greek physicians. Medicine depends on the interpretation of signs. Of course, interpretations can be mistaken – signs can be misinterpreted. This feature of signs and their interpretations can be seen particularly clearly in the case of indexical signs. The clouds may be blown elsewhere, so the rain may not arrive. A rash may currently have the appearance merely of an allergy but subsequently become typical of meningitis.

If interpretations are inherently unreliable, why do we make so much use of them? Again, indexical signs give us some clues. The reason we choose to take notice of signs is often that they are more readily accessible than the things they represent. I don't have a crystal ball that would enable me to see perfectly into the future, so I cannot predict the weather with certainty; but the presence of certain indexical signs (clouds, wind, etc.) enables me to improve my ability to predict what is likely to happen beyond the level of pure guesswork. I cannot easily examine the state of a patient's heart, but I can tell quite a lot by recording the electrical impulses detectable after placing electrodes on the skin of their chest. We use indexical signs as surrogates for more direct information. The ideal would be perfect knowledge, but we have to take the risk of being in error where perfect knowledge is impossible or impractical to obtain. In that sense, the interpretation – and misinterpretation – of indexical signs is a reflection of our finite creaturely nature. Only God is omniscient. The rest of us, in the present order of things, have to make do with fallible kinds of sign.

Signs, then, can be misleading; they can be misinterpreted. However, they are not always misleading. That may appear to be stating the obvious, but there is an influential strand of semiotic thinking that regards signs and interpretations as free-floating, operating at an entirely different level from the actual reality of things, never making contact with anything that one might call the truth. This school of semiotic thinking can arguably be traced to the work of the Swiss linguist, Ferdinand de Saussure. It had a great influence on the tone of philosophical thought in Continental Europe during the twentieth century. At risk of over-generalization, we may say that Saussure's 'semiology', in contrast to Peirce's semiotics, fails to recognize that signs and interpretations are able to connect with reality. Postmodern forms of relativism often suggest that every interpretation is as good as any other, because there is no ultimate reality against which interpretations can be checked. Or, if there is such a reality, interpretations have no purchase on it.

One antidote to this surprisingly beguiling position is the recognition of indexical forms of sign–object relation. When we think about indexical signs we can see how this particular aspect of the structure of signification is capable of connecting with reality, albeit fallibly. If I make an error of diagnosis and my patient comes to harm they will, unfortunately, not be convinced if I argue that the adverse outcome is merely a matter of interpretation. If the rash was, after all, an indication of meningitis rather than of an allergy, then the infection that I have failed to diagnose really will pose a serious danger to them. If I correctly interpret the presence of ST-segment elevation on their electrocardiogram as an early sign of a heart attack, then the action that I take really may save their life. When Thomas wanted verification of the resurrection appearances of Jesus, he stipulated that he must be able to put his finger in the marks of the nails in Jesus' hands. He was asking to see indexical signs that the risen Lord was the same man who had been crucified.

So, although signs are fallible, they do have the capacity to put us in touch with reality. We seek to refine our interpretations in order to increase the degree to which they are able to inform us about that reality. Weather forecasting is notoriously difficult. The government invests money in the Meteorological Office rather than in, say, astrology precisely because indexes – whether simple ones like the presence of clouds, or more complex ones such as the patterns of air pressure shown on weather charts – have the potential to connect our knowledge (and predictions) with the truth.

❀

Another way in which a sign can be related to an object is as a 'symbol'. In a sense, a symbol is the exact opposite of an index. Whereas an indexical sign (such as a symptom) has a direct, often causal connection with its object, a symbol has no direct connection at all with the thing it signifies. The word 'symbol' originally derives from a combination of the Greek *sun* (syn), meaning 'with', and *bole,* meaning a 'throw'. A symbolic sign is a sign that has been thrown together with its object. That is to say, a symbol could stand for anything; the fact that we take it to stand for any particular object is purely a convention. We cut with a knife and skewer with a fork. The words 'knife' and 'fork' are symbols: strings of letters with an arbitrary (though conventionally accepted) relation to the things they represent. It would be physically difficult to cut with a fork and skewer with a knife, but easy (once we got used to it) to call the sharp thing a fork and the pronged thing a knife.

In semiotic terminology, the word 'symbol' therefore has a specific meaning. This can be confusing, because in ordinary parlance 'sign' and 'symbol' are often taken to mean the same thing. In semiotics, a symbol is a particular kind of sign. We use conventional signs (symbols) all the time. Words are a familiar example, as illustrated above. Language would be very restricted without symbolic signs of this kind (knife, fork, table, chair, dog, cat, etc.). However, words are not the only kind of symbol. Shapes, colours, indeed anything, can be chosen to act as a symbolic sign. We choose red to signify 'stop' and green to signify 'go', though other colours might have served the same purpose. In the United States a $1 bill is physically quite similar to a $100 bill (confusingly so, for those of us used to recognizing the denomination of a bank note by its colour). Yet the value assigned by convention to these two green rectangles of paper with their particular numerals and decorative patterns is very different.

Why is it so important to be able to represent things with signs that have no direct relationship to their objects? We have just seen how the usefulness of indexical signs lies in their connection with reality, and this is precisely what symbolic signs lack. By definition, a symbol is a sign whose relation to its object can be arbitrary – it is not determined by any direct connection between the two. Indeed, the advantage of symbolic signs stems from precisely that fact. Because such signs are not in any way tied to their objects they can be easily manipulated; that is, they can be presented, moved around and arranged in different combinations in a way that the objects themselves cannot. If I say to you "I think I just saw the cat chasing the dog," you might reply, "No, I'm sure it was the dog chasing the cat." Using the symbols 'dog' and 'cat' enables these two scenarios to be described without recourse to the performance of an awkward sequence of mimes. Similarly, I can tell a story without having to reassemble all the people involved and physically re-enact what happened. Words are more easily corralled than people or things. Indeed, I can construct a fictional narrative by combining recognized symbols into sequences that do not match the way things have ever actually been.

Anthropologist Terrence Deacon has suggested that the capacity to use symbols is what makes humans unique.[3] The reason it is so difficult to teach language to non-human primates, he argues, is that the human mind has a very specific capacity for dissociating signs from the world and manipulating them independently of the things they represent. Perhaps the writer of the second creation account in Genesis had a similar intuition about the nature of human distinctiveness:

> So out of the ground the Lord God formed every animal of the field and every bird of the air, and brought them to the man to see what he would call them; and whatever the man called each living creature, that was its name. (Genesis 2: 19)

Humans, uniquely, make a deliberate habit of giving names – attaching symbols – to other things, animate and inanimate. I shall have more to say about the distinctiveness of human sign-use in a later chapter. At this stage it is worth flagging up what I see as a recurrent problem with the use of the term 'symbol'. I have just set out the meaning of the word symbol in the 'technical' context of the philosophy of signs (in this context, a symbol is a sign with a

---

3 Terrence Deacon, *The Symbolic Species: The Co-evolution of Language and the Human Brain* (New York and London: W. W. Norton & Co., 1997).

conventional relation to its object). But in ordinary speech the word symbol has a different meaning. Let's call this its 'folk' meaning. The folk meaning of symbol is any kind of relatively sophisticated sign. For example, certain religious practices and images are often described as forms of symbolism. Someone might say that a particular tribal ritual should be described as 'symbolic', or that the Christian Eucharist functions as a symbol. Similarly, archaeologists may refer to the intriguing female figurines fashioned by our Ice Age ancestors 20-30,000 years ago as having had 'symbolic' functions, though we can only guess at what these little sculptures signified and to whom.

These non-technical meanings of the word 'symbol' often have connotations of an almost magical function, something with the potential to connect us rather mysteriously with a hidden reality. According to Carl Jung, symbols always point to something that is ultimately beyond reason, either because they refer to some transcendent reality, or because their meaning is constructed by our unconscious. In Dan Brown's bestseller, *The Da Vinci Code*, the protagonist is a 'symbologist' whose heroic efforts to decipher a series of esoteric 'symbols' leads him to uncover a secret conspiracy at the heart of the Christian tradition. The symbologist has further work to do in a sequel, *The Lost Symbol*. Perhaps the idea that there is a special kind of sign that has a particular power to keep the truth from us has particular resonance in our current cultural situation, in which people so often feel disempowered, and standard meanings and values are so much in question. In any case, symbols, in the folk sense of the word, can be taken to be divine or diabolical, but either way there is a sense that behind their efficacy lies some kind of hidden magic or mysterious power.

There is nothing necessarily wrong with the word symbol having two different meanings. The technical and folk meanings could happily coexist if they could each agree to keep to their appropriate habitat. The technical meaning (a sign whose relation to its object is given by a rule or convention) would be at home in academic contexts, while the folk meaning would be free to spice up airport novels. The problem is that academic disciplines, including psychology, anthropology and theology, have been all too happy to adopt an essentially folk understanding of symbols. That is to say, workers in these academic fields are too ready to label something as 'symbolic' without giving a clear account of what is meant by 'symbol' (whether in accordance with the technical semiotic definition or otherwise). For example, we may like to describe the Christian Eucharist as 'symbolic', but unless we can clearly specify what we mean by this we risk making a vacuous statement. Like Molière's doctor, who attributes the sleep-inducing property of opium to the 'dormitive principle' within it, we too often implicitly accept that symbols perform their abstract representative function by virtue of some special power of, let's say, 'symbolization'. Unfortunately, this tells us nothing about how the sign in question actually works.

To put it more positively, I think we can say a lot more about religious sign-use than simply that it is 'symbolic'. Referring vaguely to the power of 'symbols' impoverishes philosophy and the human sciences because, as I shall explore towards the end of the book, I don't think our most powerful capacities for sign use depend purely on the use of symbols in the technical sense.[4] It is also bad for religion because it encourages us to think that in 'symbolic' (folk-meaning) kinds of religious representation and ritual, something essentially mysterious or magical is going on. A genuinely semiotic perspective, in contrast, will focus our attention on some quite concrete and ordinary aspects of religious practices and beliefs.

Symbologists therefore beware! Insofar as we might understand signs as mysterious, the mystery is not to be approached via the arcane and the esoteric. The true mystery would be if the basis of God's self-communication and self-revelation turned out to be, as I hope to show, the *ordinary* structure of *everyday* signs.

❀

So far we have considered two kinds of relation between signs and their objects: indexical (direct connections) and symbolic (conventional or rule-governed relations). The third way in which a sign can relate to its object is as an icon. The word derives from the Greek, *eikon*, meaning resemblance or image. An iconic sign is a sign that represents its object by resembling it in some way. A portrait represents its subject iconically because the painted image resembles the person depicted. Jesus, in Christian thinking, iconically represents God the Father: Jesus *resembles* the Father in some sense, a point to which we shall return in a later chapter when we consider the Incarnation. As Paul puts it in his letter to the Colossians (1: 15), Jesus is the image (*eikon*) of the invisible God.

---

4 In Chapter 11 I shall suggest that human distinctiveness rests on our ability to combine different kinds of sign and does not merely reflect our capacity to use one particular kind of sign-type, even symbols.

Like the word symbol, as well as its technical meaning in semiotics, icon has various less technical usages. The ordinary uses of the term have some relation to the technical meaning, but with additional connotations. We speak about people, places or events as 'iconic', meaning that they are representative, but also that they are in some way special exemplars. Marilyn Monroe was a 'Hollywood icon'. The Statue of Liberty is an 'iconic sight' at the gateway to America. Neil Armstrong stepping onto the moon was an 'iconic moment' in twentieth-century history.

In addition, in religious contexts icons are works of art of particular devotional intent and significance. They are often elaborations on standard themes such as the Madonna and Child, and are produced with particular materials according to certain stylistic conventions. At this stage, though, I would like to steer the reader away from the religious connotations of the word 'icon'. (I'm less worried about what we might call the Hollywood connotation of the term, which is unlikely to distract us too much.) Not that I have anything in principle against icons in the Byzantine sense. Undeniably, they are often beautiful and of great spiritual value. The problem with the overlap of terminology in this case is different from the problem in the case of the word 'symbol'. With symbols, the folk use of the term is too vague for our purposes. With icons, the problem is that the religious use of the word is too religious! Focussing attention on religious 'icons' might lead us to the view that certain images (icons) are especially suited to connecting us with the reality of God. Such a view might then lead us to ask, primarily, "What special kinds of image (icon) are the most effective for bringing us into God's presence?" There is nothing wrong with that, but I want to emphasize that my task is rather different. My aim, instead, is to ask how the structure of signs in general – ordinary signs as much as religious signs – is a reflection of the reality of God and the vehicle through which we encounter that reality. For that reason, I ask you to put aside the usual religious meanings that the word 'icon' may call to mind and discipline yourself to focus instead on everyday kinds of icon.

An icon in the technical semiotic sense is a sign that relates to its object by some kind of resemblance. We have seen that an obvious example is the way in which a portrait represents its subject by being a likeness of him or her. But images are not the only kind of icon. A diagram is also an iconic sign. Think, for example, of a circuit diagram. The real appearance of an electronic device may be a tangle of wires, components and connections. However, a mere photograph of the mess will not be very useful if our aim is to understand how the device works. A circuit diagram (an iconic representation of the circuit) shows the relationships between the components of the device schematically. The relationship of likeness or resemblance between the diagram and the actual object is not one of visual appearance, but of the way in which the electronic components are functionally related to one another. A metaphor is another, less obvious, kind of icon. A metaphor is a verbal image, a way of expressing something about one kind of thing in terms of its similarity (in some respect) to another kind of thing.

In some ways icons are the simplest kind of sign – they are simply *like* what they signify. But note that this 'simplicity' does not necessarily imply a lack of internal structure. Metaphors, for example, are built up from words, at least some of which will be symbolic signs. Likewise, diagrams often have symbolic elements, such as the different symbols for a capacitor and a resistor in our example of a circuit diagram. A sign of one type may thus be a composite of various signs, some being of a different kind to that of the overall sign of which they are a part. We glimpse here the way in which sign-types are not related to one another hierarchically. Rather, they mutually interpenetrate and reciprocally support one another – a characteristic which will be relevant when we come to speak of the Trinity in semiotic terms.

We saw earlier that the usefulness of indexical signs (signs directly or causally related to their objects) is that they have the capacity to connect us directly with reality. Similarly, we saw that the usefulness of symbols (signs related to their objects by convention) lies in the way they can be rearranged and combined in ways that are independent of the actual things they represent. What, then, is the particular usefulness of icons? I have probably already said enough to indicate that their utility goes beyond their capacity to be aesthetically pleasing. The example of a diagram suggests, further, that a function of icons can be to bring some specific aspect of the object in question to the forefront of attention. The circuit diagram helps us understand how an electrical device works: it is a tool that enables us to disregard certain aspects of the actual tangle of wires of which the circuit is, in reality, constructed. A diagram draws to our attention the salient features of the components and connections of the device and away from other aspects of its construction which are incidental to its function. The example of a metaphor suggests that another function of icons is to bring to light similarities between apparently different things. If I say that God is my rock, I express something about God in terms of something that is clearly not God. An icon is like its object in some respects, but unlike it in others. A portrait is like the person in certain aspects of appearance, but unlike them in being two-dimensional rather than three-dimensional.

An icon, then, has the capacity to bring to our attention certain features of the thing represented, often by excluding aspects of the object that are less relevant for the particular purpose in question. More generally, I think we could say that icons make things, or aspects of things, 'present' to us. The portrait makes the person depicted present to us even though they may be far away or long dead. The circuit diagram makes present to us important aspects of the relations between the components of the device so that we can better understand how the thing works. The metaphor makes a thing or event present to us in a fresh way, enabling us to see something about it that we might otherwise have missed or have been unable to express.

❀

To summarize, we have seen that indexes are a kind of sign that has the potential to keep our thoughts anchored in reality. Symbols, in contrast, enable us to manipulate concepts and ideas in a way that is not possible with the kinds of sign that are more directly connected with their objects. Finally, icons are forms of representation that have the capacity to make aspects of reality experientially present to us in various ways. The medium of signs, which we normally navigate so effortlessly and subconsciously, turns out, in other words, to have some kind of structure.

The full implications of this structure, and of the structure of deeper dimensions of signs, will be explored in subsequent chapters. For the moment we may think of the analysis so far as like a test-drilling through the sub-strata of signification. Our preliminary exploration has hinted that there is a deeper structure to signs than the surface features reveal. I hope that what we have turned up so far may be enough to persuade you that it is worth digging a little further.

2

Quality, Otherness and Mediation

My great grandmother used to refer to her *derrière* as her 'anatomy'. A family story relates how this had an unfortunate consequence: when my Uncle Charles was introduced socially to a professor of anatomy, he embarrassingly misunderstood the nature of the distinguished gentleman's expertise.

Some things are difficult to speak of, and confusion can arise when we attempt to do so. As Wittgenstein famously wrote, "whereof one cannot speak, thereof one must be silent." Nevertheless, in this chapter I must attempt to speak of some things with regard to which speech is, in fact, inadequate and potentially misleading. My concern is with the fundamental structure of reality – or at least, more modestly, with the deep structure of signification.

To understand the kind of thing I'd like to say about the structure of signification, consider the following analogy. Let us ask ourselves: What is the fundamental structure of music? What are the basic constituents of music, the things without which music would not be music? A musician friend tells me that the usual answer is that there are three fundamental elements to anything musical: rhythm, pitch and timbre. Rhythm is, of course, the division of notes across time. Rhythm alone, however, would not really be music. Even percussionists make use of music's other basic constituents. The second of these is pitch. Variations in pitch make it possible to play a tune. Putting these two together – rhythm and pitch – we almost have music. But not quite. You also need an instrument to play on: a piano, a flute or simply a singer's voice. Anything that can express the rhythm and the tune. What the instrument provides is the timbre – the tonal colour of the music.

Rhythm, pitch and timbre. I hope we can agree, at least for the sake of argument, that it makes sense to think of these as the most basic features of anything musical. What collective name should we give these basic building blocks of music? Constituents? Ingredients? Fundaments?[1]

---

1 The root of which is the same as the word for buttock: what everything else sits on.

I am anxious not to put the reader off by introducing anything too obscure in the way of terminology, especially as semiotics is a field already notorious for its terminological density. But I would like to find some way of labelling the idea of the underlying structure of things and a problem arises if we use terms with a well-established usage. The danger is that our understanding of reality may become shaped around the words, rather than our words shaping themselves around the nature of reality. Therefore, please forgive me for choosing what may be a slightly unfamiliar turn of phrase: I would like to refer to what gives music its basic underlying structure as its 'elemental grounds'. *Elemental* because the basic constituents of music cannot be further subdivided beyond the three we have identified. *Grounds* because these three elements provide the basis for anything and everything that can be considered musical.

The elemental grounds of music, then, are rhythm, pitch and timbre. Might it be possible to pick out something equivalent in the structure of signification?

❀

I said in the previous chapter that a sign is *something that stands for something else*. This 'something else-ness' of the sign from the object requires, as a minimum condition for the occurrence of signs, that the world is able to accommodate things that are 'other' than other things. 'Otherness' is therefore one of the elemental grounds of signification. The sign is *other* than the object. Without Otherness there could be no representation, no signification, because nothing could ever stand for something *else*.

I have already suggested that the elemental grounds of music are rhythm, pitch and timbre. Importantly, although rhythm, pitch and timbre are fundamental to the nature of music, they can also be noticed in other phenomena that are not normally considered musical. I may, for example, notice a certain rhythm to the tapping noises that sometimes emanate from the old water pipes in our house, or I may notice the wind humming through telephone wires at a certain pitch, even though neither of these phenomena are musical as such. Similarly, it should not surprise us that the Otherness that separates the sign from its object may also be discerned in aspects of the world that are not obviously involved in any process of signification. Just look around you and notice *difference*: two different objects, or two different colours, or a boundary between one thing or colour and another. These simple differences – the 'this-not-that' elements of everyday experience – are manifestations of the elemental ground I am calling Otherness.

At an even more personal, experiential level, we meet Otherness whenever the world seems to resist us or constrain us. If I stub my toe, I encounter something that is other than me, and its otherness causes me pain. If I earnestly desire something and am disappointed that it does not come about, I similarly confront the otherness of the world's being from my own. If such instances of Otherness did not exist, we would float through the world as if it were some kind of airy nothingness. We would never be constrained or impeded, challenged or surprised. A little thought will quickly show that while this might guarantee that we would never again stub a toe it would also mean that our selfhood – if it could exist at all – would be of a kind that could never go anywhere, do anything or signify anything. All processes of cause and effect would cease to operate. Billiard balls would float through one another rather than colliding and being deflected, their otherness no longer real. Without Otherness, the world would be a more comfortable place, but it would also be a place without the possibility of direction or change, and without the possibility of one thing standing for another thing. That is, it would be devoid of signification and meaning.

Later in this chapter we will begin to put together a way of speaking about the Trinity using what we uncover about the structure of signs and the elemental grounds that underpin that structure. I see no point in being coy, however, about where the present line of thought will eventually lead. For now we may note that the Christian tradition has come to speak of the eternal being of God in terms of the Father and the Son (and, of course, the Spirit). An important trajectory in early Christian thought, culminating in the creeds of the fourth century, was the recognition of the equality of Father and Son. But, however much we want to say that the Father and Son have in common, it has never been orthodox to say that the Father *is* the Son or the Son *is* the Father. The tradition has always held that the Son is other than the Father.[2]

Otherness, then, is an aspect of the eternal being of God. One of the things I want to invite you to consider is that the Otherness we experience in the world is somehow a reflection of the Otherness that is within God, the Otherness of Father from Son.

But I jump ahead of myself; let us return to the remaining elemental grounds of signification.

2 I should make clear that I have no interest in defending orthodoxy for orthodoxy's sake. Orthodoxy is only of interest to the extent that it 'works'; that is, if it helps to provide a coherent framework within which to pursue the calling of Christian discipleship.

❀

In addition to the nature of the relation between the sign and the object (which rests on Otherness), the full structure of signification also depends on whomever or whatever interprets the sign. I will have more to say about the nature of interpretation later. For the moment, we need to see that the sign works, in some way, by *coming between* the object and the interpreter. When a sign is standing for an object the interpreter does not encounter the object directly. Rather, the interpreter encounters the sign, which in some way *stands in* for the object. For example, if I see pictures of various kinds of ice-cream cone and lolly in the window of an ice-cream van, I do not encounter the ice creams themselves (which need to be kept in the freezer), but images of those ice creams that connect me to the actual cold-and-tasty objects of my desire.

We may therefore say that the sign *mediates* between the object and the interpreter. In that sense, signification depends on the elemental ground of 'Mediation'. You can't get true mediation by any amount of combining instances of Otherness any more than you can get pitch or timbre by elaborating a series of rhythms. A sign can't mediate between the object and the interpreter without the underlying element of Mediation – the possibility of something joining two 'others' together into a new kind of whole. The picture of the ice cream joins me to something currently invisible – the real ice cream – in a way that leads me to a previously unrealized understanding: namely, the imminent possibility of consuming an actual Double 99.

As with Otherness, Mediation can be found in the world even apart from its specific role in the structure of signs. Perhaps we most often think of mediation in a personal sense, as when a mediator tries to bring two sides together in a negotiation. But mediation can also be noted at more basic levels of experience. Two dots on a piece of paper are simply 'other' than one another. But a third dot between them begins to make a line (if you think the two dots themselves imply a line you are already imagining the third dot, and others). Indeed, a line is a form of continuum: a continuous sequence of points in which, if any two points are chosen (however close together), there is always another point mediating between them, connecting them up.

We can see, then, that there can be nothing genuinely connected about the world without the operation of Mediation. Such connectivity does not always take the form of concrete, physical things like lines and dots. When a thought makes a link between two things (or between other thoughts), a form of Mediation is in play.

Similarly, an idea or concept reflects a kind of continuity which, like a continuum of dots, requires Mediation to be in action. For example, a mouse, an elephant and a dinosaur are all animals. There is nothing, however, that is simply 'animal' in the world. Rather, 'animal' is a concept that ties together and mediates between all individual instances of things that are animals.

The theological correlate of Mediation, I suggest, is the role of the Spirit within the eternal Trinity. The Spirit mediates between the Father and the Son, and this action is mirrored in the way that Mediation operates in the world. More precisely, when a sign mediates between the object and the interpreter, the elemental ground of Mediation is in operation; just as when the Word represents the Father to us, he does so through the work of the Spirit as the ground of mediation.

⚜

If the relationship between the sign and the object manifests Otherness, and if the sign functions to mediate between the object and interpreter, requiring the existence of an elemental ground that we are calling Mediation, what about the object itself? The object, considered in itself, manifests the elemental ground I am going to call Quality. An object has certain qualities. For example, a table can be flat, hard, stable, and so on. The object can also have a certain overall 'quality' constituted by the sum of all these separate qualities. The table's 'quality' is what the table is *in itself*.[3] Of course when I speak of the 'quality' of the table I'm speaking of something broader than just its worth or value. A rickety table may not have much 'quality' in the sense of usefulness, but its ricketiness is nevertheless an aspect of the elemental ground of Quality.

The cardinal feature of Quality, then, is a certain sort of 'in-itself-ness'. We experience something of the elemental ground named Quality when, for example, we contemplate a particular colour: the blueness of this particular blue or the redness of that particular red. In experiencing the colour we are, in part, experiencing its Otherness, in the sense that we experience it as different from the surrounding colours and context. But if we strip away that aspect of the experience, the otherness of whatever we are presented with, and instead allow ourselves to become immersed in the colour itself, then we touch on Quality in its fundamental, elemental sense.

---

3 The same could be said about the sign-in-itself, but we will leave the consideration of this until Chapter 4.

Experiencing Quality is like peeling away the layers of an onion; in our moment-to-moment experience of the world all the fundamental elements, the elemental grounds, are always in play. But if we make the effort to strip away the layers of the structure of experience, what we are left with when it seems that no more stripping away is possible is Quality. Quality is like a feeling; indeed, feelings are themselves aspects of Quality. What we experience when we experience a feeling or an emotion can, if we want to help others know what we are talking about, be given a label. But ultimately the feeling or emotion, as experienced, cannot adequately be translated into anything else. It simply *is what it is*: and, as such, it is a manifestation of Quality.

By a process of elimination, if in no other way, you will see that the theological correlate of Quality within the eternal being of God in this analysis is the Father. The Father is the one whose being does not come directly from or through any of the other persons. The Father, to use a technical theological term, is 'unbegotten'. That, as we shall see, does not make the Father superior to the other persons. It doesn't even mean that the Father could have his being without the other persons. But it does make the Father's personhood distinctive, just as the other persons have their distinctive characters of Otherness and Mediation.

❀

As a way into thinking about the fundamental underlying structure of signs and signification, I therefore offer three basic elements of reality that seem to be necessary to the processes of representation and interpretation. These elemental grounds are Quality, Otherness and Mediation.

I have no intention of attempting to prove to you that Quality, Otherness and Mediation are indeed the elemental grounds of signification. Still less am I setting out to persuade you (as I have been hinting) that they might, more than this, be the elemental grounds of reality itself. However, I will not attempt to conceal the fact that, having seen the world through the lens of this threefold dynamic for a number of years, I am inclined to entertain such thoughts. By the end of this book you may or may not share my opinion of the fundamental nature of these grounds of signification. If you do not – if you decide that this is just one way of seeing the world among others – so be it. I think you may still find something of value in what I am going to say, although you may reach a different understanding of certain ideas that I shall be exploring in later chapters; ideas, for example, about participation in the divine nature, or the possibility that there are 'vestiges of the Trinity' in creation.

You will have noticed, I expect, that as we consider the way in which the grounding elements of reality play out in the structure of signs, I will indicate that I am referring to an elemental ground by capitalizing it. Quality will refer to the element that underlies all particular instances of in-itself-ness. Likewise, Otherness will refer to the element that underpins all particular instances of otherness and difference. Mediation will refer to the element that is the ground of all particular instances of mediation and connection. Notice also that when I use one of the capitalized names it will sometimes (as in the last few sentences) be sufficient for me to shorten 'elemental ground' to 'element', since the context will make it clear that 'element' is being used as a shorthand for 'elemental ground'.

As a further way of identifying the elemental grounds, one that will become helpful when we start looking at how they can combine, let me suggest that we represent each of them with a shape:

◯ *Quality*   ▢ *Otherness*   △ *Mediation*

The circle will stand for Quality, representing the unitary character of in-itself-ness. The square will stand for Otherness; think, perhaps, of the *opposition* of the pairs of parallel sides to each other, or the *difference* in direction of the lines as they turn the right-angles. The triangle will stand for Mediation, reminding us of the 'third' – any one of the three sides – that comes between and connects two 'others' in any instance of mediatory function.

Using this visual notation let us summarize what has been discussed so far about the role of the three elemental grounds within the overall structure of any sign and its interpretation:

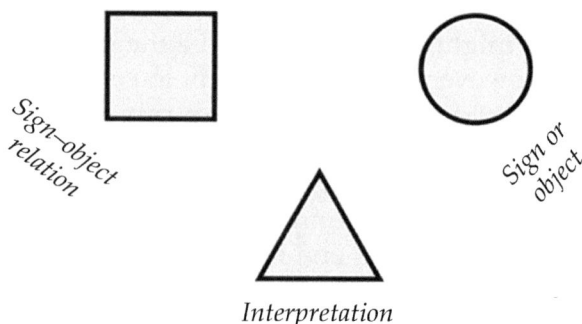

Interpretation

The diagram expresses the fact that the overall structure of signification – sign, object, interpretation – seems to require that the world is able to accommodate the occurrence of qualities (what something is in itself), otherness (one thing being different from another) and mediation (something coming between and connecting two other things). The object depends on and is a manifestation of the elemental ground of Quality, depicted by the circle. The sign–object relation depends on and is a manifestation of the elemental ground of Otherness, depicted by the square. And the mediation of the sign between object and interpreter depends on and is a manifestation of the elemental ground of Mediation, depicted by the triangle.

It is worth noting in passing that at least two of these aspects of signification are not 'things', but relations. So the square (Otherness) corresponds not to the sign or object itself, but to the sign–object relation. The triangle (Mediation) corresponds not to the interpreter but to the interpretation, which, as we have seen, involves the sign coming to mediate between the object and the interpreting person or agent. Even the circle (Quality, the ground of the in-itself-ness of the object or sign) cannot be thought of outside the context of these relations, for it represents the element characterized by being neither of these kinds of relation.

This inherent relationality is a promising start when it comes to thinking about the Trinity in semiotic terms. Specifically, I shall be inviting you to consider that the pattern of relations that underpins every event of representation and interpretation may offer a way of thinking about the eternal threefold being of God. In other words, I will be outlining a 'semiotic model' of the Trinity.

❀

To flesh out this semiotic model of the Trinity, we could do worse than to compare my thesis with St Augustine's reflections on the Trinity in the early fifth century. I acknowledge that there are many theologians who think Augustine's thought *is* the worst place to start! I happen to think they are wrong, but in any case my purpose here is not to defend Augustine's account, but to use it as a vehicle to explore the 'semiotic model' of the Trinity.

Those who already know of Augustine's efforts to seek likenesses of the Trinity in the world (and it doesn't matter if you do not) will probably know that his approach is usually summarized with reference to his various 'triads'. One of these is the triad of memory, understanding and will. A related one is that of mind, knowledge and love.[4] In the conceptual space around these triads, however,

---

4 Augustine's exploration of likenesses of the Trinity can be found in Books VIII-XV of *The Trinity*. Book XV is a good place to start for an overview of the position he reaches.

Augustine sets out some ideas that are even more fundamental to his trinitarian thinking than the triads themselves. These ideas, at least as I read Augustine, open up an explicitly semiotic perspective on God's triune being. The first of these principles is that words or thoughts are "utterances of the heart." The second is that the Spirit is the love that binds together the Father and Son. The third is that nothing can be loved that is not already known.

Consider, then, the first principle: that words or thoughts are "utterances of the heart." What does Augustine mean by this? Not, I think, that everything we say is always sincere, or that what we say always springs from our emotions. Rather, Augustine's starting point is that there is always a mass of things that we know, but that we are not currently thinking about. The fact that we can think about these things if we want to shows that we must in some sense know them, but, until we are thinking about them, they are invisible and formless. This subconscious store of knowledge is what Augustine refers to as mind, memory or, in the phrase we are focussing on, the heart.

If this mass of things that we know is mostly below the level of conscious thought, how does it become available to our conscious mind? Augustine's answer is that, in order to turn our attention to something we unconsciously know, we need to form our unarticulated knowledge into words. These words are the utterances of our heart. They are not necessarily words spoken out loud; they are the silent words that make up our thoughts, our internal conversation with ourselves.[5] However, we are free to share our thoughts with others by speaking outwardly, so the utterances of our hearts may become more widely known.

Augustine's idea is that the relation between the mass of unspoken knowledge that we hold in our memories, and the silent internal words by which that knowledge comes to be articulated, is analogous to the relationship between the Father and the Son. The Father is unseen, unknown and in some sense unknowable in himself. But the Father eternally utters the Son/Word, and it is through the Word that the Father has an eternal and perfect kind of self-knowledge. In the familiar opening words of John's Gospel, "In the beginning was the Word, and the Word was with God, and the Word was God. He was in the beginning with God" (John 1: 1-2).

---

5 A common criticism of Augustine's account is that it allegedly leads to a view of the human mind as isolated and autonomous, rather than being formed by participation in the social structures of language. I shall attempt to show why the semiotic model of the Trinity is not vulnerable to such criticisms in Chapter 5.

To extend the analogy: in ordinary experience, if we want to communicate our thoughts to others, we have to turn our internal speech into something external and physical – words or gestures of a kind that can be seen and understood. In the same way, for the Father's hidden self to be communicated to his creation, his eternal Word must become embodied in a form that is accessible to us. Hence the pivotal assertion of John's prologue: "And the Word became flesh" (John 1: 14). This embodied Word, God's outward speech, communicates to us the character of God's inner being. Similarly, the opening claim in the first chapter of Colossians, the beautiful summary of Christ's cosmic role of reconciliation, is that, "He is the *image* of the invisible God" (Colossians 1: 15). Of course, reconciliation on a cosmic scale does not come about through the presentation by the Father of a partial image, nor by means of a flippant word or casual remark. The Word faithfully represents the entirety of God's being, "For in him all the fullness of God was pleased to dwell" (Colossians 1: 19). As the writer of the letter to the Hebrews puts it, "He is the radiance of God's glory, the stamp of God's very being" (Hebrews 1: 3; Revised English Bible).

❀

I hope I do not have to work too hard to persuade you that all of this is very much consonant with what we have already seen about the structure of signs. The object has an 'in-itself-ness' grounded in the elemental ground that we have called Quality, an in-itself-ness that exists prior to the object being represented in any way. When the object comes to be represented by the sign, the sign is something other than the object. The sign–object relation is grounded in the elemental ground of Otherness. Quality and Otherness are both necessary for something to be represented by something else. A word is an utterance of the heart, and however closely and fully it expresses what is in the heart it is still something that stands, in its Otherness, as separate from the 'heart'. The Word is everything that the Father is, except that he is not the Father.

Note that there is a logical order of trinitarian persons in this discussion, although in the case of God's threefold nature there is not, of course, a hierarchy of levels of being. A word is 'born' of the formless mass of our mind; the eternal Word is begotten from the unbegotten being of the Father. But, just as being born does not make the child a lesser being than the parent, being uttered does not necessarily make the Word a lesser being than that which it represents. Neither is the Word diminished when it is spoken out loud; the eternal Word is still the Word, even when it is enfleshed in the world.

Augustine is at pains to emphasize the great dissimilarities between the things that he identifies in the world as showing triadic likenesses to the being of God and the original three-ness of God's triune being. But it would be a mistake to think that Augustine is thereby backing away from the claim that these likenesses are in some way true likenesses of God. Rather, when he qualifies the status of the likeness, he always makes a distinction between something that operates in a particular way in finite creatures and the same basic pattern as it subsists within the non-finite Creator of everything.

A parallel set of qualifications may be made in the context of the semiotic model:

- In the world, objects are things that exist alongside other things; insofar as the Father can be analogously referred to as the 'object' of a sign, he 'exists' as the ground of the possibility of *all* existence.
- In the world, something's existence usually precedes its representation; in God, the Word represents the Father *eternally*, without beginning or end.
- In the world, something usually represents something else in some respect but not in others; in God the Word perfectly represents the Father in *every* respect.
- In the world, or in our minds, our representations of things and situations may be complex, muddled, and changing; in God the eternal representation of the Father need consist of only *one perfect utterance.*
- In the world, signs are often misinterpreted; within the being of God, the Word's representation of the Father is *never fallible.*

❀

This latter point brings us to the question of the role of the Spirit. As I have suggested, the second overall principle in Augustine's view of the Trinity is that the Spirit binds together, or joins in communion, the Father and Son. Let us note, crucially, that this immediately suggests a connection between the Spirit and our elemental ground of Mediation. In John V. Taylor's memorable phrase, the Spirit is the "Go-Between-God."[6] Interestingly, in ancient Greek the word *paraclete*, which Jesus uses to name the Spirit in John's Gospel and which is usually translated as 'advocate' or 'helper', can also mean 'mediator'.

6 John V. Taylor, *The Go-Between God: The Holy Spirit and the Christian Mission* (London: SCM Press, 1972). Interestingly, Taylor's position in *The Christ-Like God* (London: SCM Press 1992) fits well with my discussion of the Incarnation in Chapter 4.

As we have already seen, the role of Mediation in the process of signification is rather subtle. Although the elemental ground of Mediation is required in order for a sign to be meaningful to an interpreter, it is the sign itself that does the mediating. That is why it is not surprising that Scripture refers to Christ as the mediator. But that does not make the Word the ground of mediation. The elemental ground of Mediation – the ground of the possibility of mediation – is the work of the Spirit. I believe it makes sense, therefore, to speak of the Spirit as the divine interpreter of the Word. Without the Spirit grounding the meaningfulness of the Word, there would be no interpretation of the Word within the eternal being of God. This interpretative role is reflected in the Spirit's activity in the world. The central biblical event supporting this view is Pentecost, the inauguration of the church, when the activity of the Spirit enabled people from all the nations under heaven each to hear (interpret) the gospel in their own language.

We should briefly note that there has been much theological hand-wringing in contemporary trinitarian thought over the apparent neglect of the Spirit: her tendency to be overlooked alongside the other two (traditionally male) persons of the Trinity. Feminist theologians have done much to diagnose and rectify this situation. I would hazard a guess, though, that an under-appreciated reason for the neglect of the Spirit is the failure of the Western philosophical tradition to recognize the fundamental nature of Mediation. Or, rather, perhaps the problem is that the tradition has never managed to come to terms with how to acknowledge the enduring reality of Otherness *and* the real operation of continuity (Mediation) without allowing one of them to subsume the other. In any case, without an appreciation of the metaphysical distinctiveness of the Spirit and her specific role as the eternal interpreter of the Word – the mediator and ground of mediation, who energizes the eternal dynamic of meaning – it is not surprising that the Spirit's full equality with the Father and Son has been hard to articulate.

❀

Augustine, it has to be said, does not explicitly link what he says about the Spirit as mediator to any notion of a role for the Spirit in the eternal *interpretation* of the Word. Instead he goes to considerable lengths to justify a connection between the Holy Spirit and the operation of *love* or the *will* within the human mind. Does anything further connect Augustine's approach to mine regarding the Spirit? And if so, does this give us any useful insights into how to think about the Trinity in semiotic terms?

Recall for a moment Augustine's most commonly cited triadic formulations. The first element is the memory (or mind), the formless unarticulated store of things that we know. The second element is understanding or knowledge: knowledge articulated (inwardly or outwardly) as thoughts or words. The third element is love, or the will. For Augustine, knowledge and understanding are somehow incomplete if not met by a response of love or an effort of the will. The key thing here, I think, is that the third element of the triad is some kind of attentiveness or response to what is articulated in the second element. We respond to a word or thought by a movement of love, or by the directed effort of our willed intentions, or by both of these.

The connection between this and the semiotic model, I suggest, lies in the nature of interpretation. An interpretation is always a response of some kind; a response, that is, to a sign. We shall see in Chapter 3 that interpretations can be thoughts, feelings, or actions. Although we normally think of interpretation as a *conscious* activity of the mind, conscious thought is therefore not the only form of interpretation. The key point for the moment is that an interpretation is some sort of response. This means that an interpretation always changes the interpreter in some way. A feeling is present that was not experienced until then; an action is performed that takes the interpreter from one state to another; a thought arises that directs the interpreter to some other thought or thing not previously being attended to.

These kinds of interpretative response encompass the whole of creaturely existence. If we were to respond to something in all three of these ways, with our feelings, actions and thoughts, the holistic nature of our response would be a reflection of the engagement of our whole self with the object of our attention. When Augustine speaks of love or the will as the third element of his triad, I think he may be touching on a similar idea. The third element, love or will, is an attentive purposeful response to the articulated Word. It is only in the context of such a response – which in the semiotic model is understood as an *interpretative* response – that the Father and the Word uttered by the Father are fully joined together.

To summarize this in a brief formula, we could say that *God's life is the Spirit's eternal interpretation of the Word as a perfect sign of the Father*. This way of putting it will be important when we consider (in Chapter 6) how we creatures may be caught up in the trinitarian dynamic by ourselves becoming interpreters of the Word.

❀

God's life is the Spirit's eternal interpretation of the Word as a perfect sign of the Father. On the face of it this formula may seem to run the risk of making interpretation more important than love. In other words, it may seem an overly intellectual way of picturing the Trinity. I must explain two things to fend off such a suspicion at this stage. The first is that love will reappear in my narrative as the very quality of God's eternal being. Second, it will be central to everything I am going to say about interpretations that, although we may tend to think of them in intellectual terms, they encompass the whole range of emotional and bodily responses (feelings and actions as well as thoughts). Such responses are not necessarily coldly intellectual or rational; indeed, in our everyday navigation of the sea of signs around us, they are rarely so.

A further apparent problem is that Augustine's way of putting things may seem to make the third element of the triad rather incidental to the other two. The problem becomes acute if we isolate Augustine's final principle (to which we will now turn) from its wider context. This third principle, as I mentioned earlier, is that nothing can be loved that is not already known. But if that is the case, while there is a very intimate relation between the Father and the Word that he utters, the Spirit can apparently only be involved after the Word has been uttered, since before that nothing is known about the Father and therefore nothing can be loved.

One response to this, of course, would be to point out that all talk of 'before' and 'after' in relation to the Spirit's interpretation of the uttered Word is entirely metaphorical, because there is no before and after in God's eternal being. There is perhaps an even more important kind of response that can be made, however, one that is suggested in Augustine's own meditations on the problem. The clue is in the qualifications that Augustine finds it necessary to add to his assertion that nothing can be loved unless it is known. If that is so, he asks, why do we seek any kind of knowledge in the first place? If we do not have a sense that what we are seeking is to be desired (loved), even though we do not yet know in full what it is that we are going to love, why embark on any kind of pursuit of the unknown? The explanation offered is that we already know enough about the subject in question to know that further knowledge is desirable. Hence, love plays a part in seeking and acquiring knowledge; it is not limited to being a response that we make only once we are fully in possession of such knowledge.

When we attend to and respond to the world in order to learn more about it, we, in a sense, invite it to speak about itself. Even more obviously, if we wish someone to speak about themselves, we will need to direct our own loving attention to them. When they sense that we genuinely desire them to speak their own words, then they may begin to tell us what is on their mind. Similarly, but perhaps requiring even more practice, if we want to learn about ourselves, we need to learn to switch off our constant internal chatter and be attentive to whatever may unexpectedly appear from within.

Subject to the necessary caveats listed above (p. 26) concerning the great divide between creature and Creator, this example is the one closest to God's inner self. Within the being of God there is no 'other' whose speech is awaited. The only one capable of utterance is the Father. And yet we need not imagine that the Spirit is waiting passively for this utterance, only able to participate once the Word has emerged. Augustine acknowledges that there is an inquisitiveness or appetite involved in bringing forth knowledge (*The Trinity*, IX.3). In this sense knowledge (speech, the Word) is born (begotten) whereas the appetite or love (Spirit) that brings it to birth is not begotten (otherwise the Father would have two children). One might say that the Spirit is midwife to the birth of the Word. Hence, I think it is possible to understand the interpretative role of the Spirit not merely in the passive sense of responding to the Word once it is born or expressed, but as actively involved in inviting, attending to and responding to the birthing of the Father's utterance. If the Spirit is not simply the mediator, but also the ground of the possibility of mediation, then the Spirit's role is not just to interpret what has already been spoken, but also to coax and elicit from within the depths of being the utterance of the Word that is to be interpreted.

All of this implies a kind of mutual interdependence of Father, Son and Spirit, so that none can be envisaged as containing the fullness of their being apart from their relations with the other two. The Word is uttered by the Father, but its utterance is dependent on, and elicited by, the Father's anticipation of its interpretation by the Spirit. The Father is logically prior to the Word in that he, the Father, is the utterer, but without the Word the Father would be unknown and unknowable, even to himself. Without the Father and the Word there would be nothing for the Spirit to mediate between. But without the possibility of mediation and interpretation, the Father would not utter and the Word would not be uttered.

❀

In this chapter I have introduced the idea that the structure of signs is underpinned by three 'elemental grounds': Quality, Otherness and Mediation. Reflection on Augustine's account of the Trinity has helped us to see how Quality relates to the 'unbegotten' character of the Father, how Otherness correlates with the relation between the Father and the Son, and how Mediation corresponds to the activity of the Spirit. According to this semiotic model of the Trinity, the Spirit is the eternal interpreter of the Word, the Word being the perfect representation of the Father.

This is an appropriate juncture at which to point out something important about the use of names to label the elemental grounds. The problem is that trying to name or define the fundamental structures of signification can never really work. It's like asking a group of musicians to name the elements of music using only the sounds they can make with their instruments. Of course they could give examples of rhythm, pitch and timbre, but that is not the same as naming or defining them. Likewise, for example, to give a name to the element associated with the phenomenon of 'in-itself-ness' is already to add something to that 'in-itself-ness', thereby disrupting its very character. Pointing to the in-itself-ness of something by using the label Quality, or indeed any other name or description, can only ever amount to a vague gesture towards the actual elemental ground in question; it can never be a precise or final definition. The same problem applies to all three of the elemental grounds, though the problem is perhaps most easily appreciated in the case of Quality.

Since the naming of the trinitarian persons is, understandably, a touchy subject in some circles, this is as good a place as any to say that for convenience I will continue to use the traditional names of Father, Son and Spirit for the three eternal persons of the Trinity. That is not, however, because I think these names are entirely unproblematic, and it certainly does not imply that I wish to dismiss discussion of the subject altogether. My discussion of the Trinity already contains much that may appear new or unfamiliar without compounding the difficulty by attempting to rename the trinitarian persons. If naming the elemental grounds of signification within the world turns out to be a hopeless – though unavoidable – task, how much more unsatisfactory must it be to try to name without distortion (or to take the traditional names as unproblematic descriptions of) the three eternal grounds of the very being of God?

3

The Dance of Meaning

Rhythm, pitch and timbre are the elemental grounds of music. Using this as an analogy, I suggested in the previous chapter that Quality, Otherness and Mediation are the three basic elements in the structure of signification, corresponding to the object, the sign–object relation, and the interpretation of the sign. These initial thoughts about the nature of representation were developed into what I call a 'semiotic model' of the Trinity. Before we can explore this semiotic model more fully, we must undertake some further analysis of the structure of signs.

Let me suppose, for a moment, that you are of a sceptical turn of mind. It doesn't prove much, you may say, just to show that those three things – Quality, Otherness and Mediation – help to describe the overall relation between these key aspects of the semiotic triad. You are prepared to grant that the object, the sign–object relation, and the interpretation may fit such a pattern. But you may want to insist (and I think you would be right to do so) that you must see further evidence of the elemental grounds at work in the processes of representation and interpretation before you will accept that they are in some way fundamental to signification.

At this stage, the musical analogy breaks down slightly. In music, we would certainly doubt that rhythm, pitch and timbre were true elemental grounds if they turned out to apply to classical music but not, say, to blues or jazz. That they are in fact necessary to these and other forms of music is what makes it plausible to consider them the basic elements of anything musical. In relation to signification, I would like you to see that the elements of Quality, Otherness and Mediation do not just underpin every instance of representation, whether artistic, literary, scientific and so on – equivalent to blues, jazz and classical music in the analogy. I want to invite you to see, also, that the same elements penetrate *other dimensions* of the processes of signification in a way for which there is no direct analogy in the analysis of music.

To undertake this further examination of the structure of signs, we must return to what we saw in the first chapter about the various kinds of relation between signs and the objects they represent. Recall that there are three such kinds of sign–object relation: iconic, indexical and symbolic. The first kind, an icon, is a sign that is related to its object by some kind of resemblance. Another way of putting this is to say that the icon and the object have some kind of *quality* in common. They do not normally share every quality: icons usually resemble their objects in some respects but not others. A portrait is two-dimensional not three-dimensional; a circuit diagram won't actually function as an electrical device; a metaphor will malfunction if it is taken too literally. As we shall see in Chapter 4, there is one kind of icon in which the sign resembles the object in *all* respects: the sign is nothing other than the quality it represents. For the moment, however, the important point is that an icon works by resembling its object in some way, not necessarily in every way. In other words, an icon *re*-presents some quality of the object.

We may therefore say that iconic representation depends on, and is underpinned by, the element of Quality.

An index, as we have seen, is a sign that represents its object by virtue of some kind of direct or causal relationship between the two. Earlier I used the example of a medical symptom. Another standard example is a weathervane. The weathervane is a sign of the direction of the wind because the wind pushes the pointer in whatever direction it happens to be blowing. Of course the wind has no thought of doing so, it simply has that effect. A leaf blown along the ground in the breeze would similarly be an indexical sign. Indexes work because of some kind of direct encounter between sign and object. It is this *otherness* of the object from the sign that accounts for the object's capacity to impinge on the sign, or which characterizes the causal relation between the two.

The exact nature of the direct connection between indexical sign and object varies. We saw that a cloud is a sign of possible rain because clouds hold the water that may fall as precipitation. Clouds turn into rain. The relevant otherness here is between two different forms in which the water may exist and the causal connection between them. Clouds are a sign of possible rain because one form, in certain circumstances, is caused to be converted into the other. Similarly, a footprint on the carpet is a sign that someone came in with muddy shoes. The sign arises because of the otherness between the clean carpet and the muddy sole. The one impresses itself directly on the other. In these, and all other varieties of indexical sign, it is some kind of direct connection between two things (such as between a cause and its effect) that characterizes the sign–object relationship.

As we have seen in the previous chapter, when one thing comes up against, impinges upon, or causes something else, the elemental ground of Otherness is at play. It follows that indexical sign–object relations depend on, and are underpinned by, the element of Otherness.

Finally, symbols are signs that are connected with their objects by a convention or rule. There are various road signs in and around my home town of Newton Abbot that include, alongside pointers to surrounding towns and villages, some apparently meaningless coloured shapes – a green circle, a red square, a blue diamond and so on. On their own, these shapes would provide no useful information. After a while, however, one notices that their meaning is given on a series of large signboards on the roads leading into the town. These are headed "Newton Abbot Industrial Estates: Follow Symbol." Below this instruction is the key to the relevant correspondences: Bradley Lane – green circle; Milber – yellow star; Decoy Industrial Estate – blue diamond. Thus we are provided with the rules that connect the symbols with their object. Without the rule, there would be no connection between a blue diamond and the industrial units at Decoy. And I salute the sign-maker who devised this scheme and correctly identified it as symbolic. For it is not symbolic in the folk sense, but in the technical semiotic sense.

Now the rule or convention that connects a symbol with its object *mediates* between the two. It joins together two things that were previously unconnected. It is evident, therefore, that symbolic signs depend on, and are underpinned by, the element of Mediation.

❀

We begin to see, then, how the elements of Quality, Otherness and Mediation seem to appear in more than one layer of the structure of signs. For the sign–object relation we can depict this as follows:

Sign–object relation

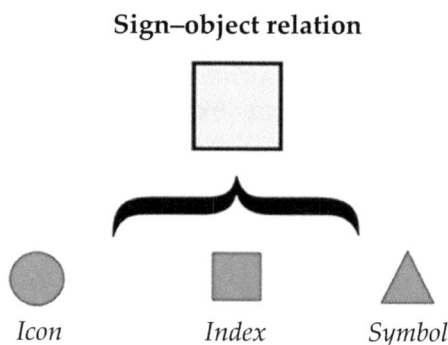

Icon   Index   Symbol

The diagram reminds us that the sign–object relation is a manifestation of Otherness, hence the large overarching square at the top of the diagram – the otherness of the sign from the object. But we have seen that there are three distinct kinds of sign–object relation. Icons depend primarily on the element of Quality, indexes depend primarily on the element of Otherness, and symbols depend primarily on the element of Mediation. Below the overarching large square the full set of elemental grounds therefore recurs at another level: the small circle, square and triangle.

It seems, therefore, that Quality, Otherness and Mediation are operative both at the level of the overall structure of signification (sign, sign–object relation and interpretation) and in at least one other dimension of the structure of signs, namely the various kinds of sign–object relation. But if sign–object relations may be subdivided into three kinds, each corresponding to one of the elemental grounds, might the same be true of interpretations? In that case, just like the diagram above representing icons, indexes and symbols, we might expect to be able to tease out the following pattern for interpretations:

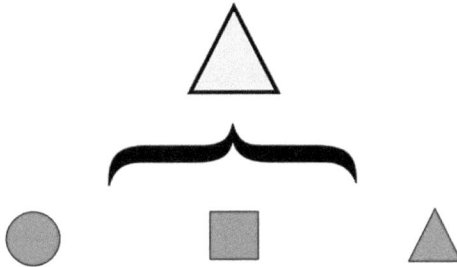

As we have seen in Chapter 2, interpretation as a whole involves Mediation: the sign comes to mediate between the object and the interpreting agent. Hence the large triangle at the top of the diagram. Within this overall dimension of interpretation we look for three distinct modes of interpretation, corresponding to Quality, Otherness and Mediation.

You may recall that I previously mentioned three kinds of interpretative response: feelings, actions and thoughts. Let me therefore set you a little task. Each of the Gospel passages below includes a reference to one of these three subtypes of interpretation. The exercise is to see whether you can pick out the three different kinds of interpretative response in the Gospel verses. A further task is to identify which type of interpretative response corresponds to each of the elemental grounds. In other words, what is the correspondence between Quality, Otherness and Mediation (the small circle, square and triangle in the diagram above) and interpretative thoughts, feelings and actions?

The Pharisees and Sadducees came, and to test Jesus they asked him to show them a sign from heaven. He answered them, "When it is evening, you say, 'It will be fair weather, for the sky is red.' And in the morning, 'It will be stormy today, for the sky is red and threatening.' You know how to interpret the appearance of the sky, but you cannot interpret the signs of the times." (Matthew 16: 1-3)

And Jesus went with them, but when he was not far from the house, the centurion sent friends to say to him, "Lord, do not trouble yourself, for I am not worthy to have you come under my roof; therefore I did not presume to come to you. But only speak the word, and let my servant be healed. For I also am a man set under authority, with soldiers under me; and I say to one, 'Go', and he goes, and to another 'Come', and he comes, and to my slave, 'Do this', and the slave does it." (Luke 7: 6-8)

When Mary came where Jesus was and saw him, she knelt at his feet and said to him, "Lord, if you had been here, my brother would not have died." When Jesus saw her weeping, and the Jews who came with her also weeping, he was greatly disturbed in spirit and deeply moved. (John 11: 32-33)

❀

How did you do? Have you managed to identify interpretative feelings, thoughts and actions in these passages? And have you thought about how these correlate with the elemental grounds of Quality, Otherness and Mediation? Here are the answers I had in mind:

△ *The sign from heaven: interpretative thoughts*

In this passage, Jesus asks the Pharisees and Sadducees to imagine themselves interpreting the colour of the sky with a *thought*. If they saw that the sky was a red colour in the evening he suggests that they would *say to themselves* (i.e. think), "It will be fair weather, for the sky is red." Interestingly, note that essentially the same sign requires a different thought to interpret it in a different context. If the red sky occurred in the morning rather than the evening, the thought would be: "It will be stormy today, for the sky is red and threatening."

   Thoughts are the form of interpretation that depend on and manifest the element of Mediation. This is because, as I alluded to earlier, thoughts connect one thing with another thing (the 'things' here could be other thoughts). In the red sky example, the thought connects the sign (the present perception of the red sky) with a body of experience (when the sky is red in the evening the weather is usually fine the following day). This connection is reflected in the little word 'for' in each of the key sentences in the passage. We expect X 'for' (i.e. because) we have seen Y.

One might easily assume that *all* interpretations are thoughts. This would reflect an anthropocentric bias, according to which only rational creatures are presumed to be capable of interpreting signs. One of the insights of the school of semiotic theory deriving from C.S. Peirce is that interpretation is not always a matter of reasoned thought or argument. Interpretations can be embedded much more deeply in human experience and behaviour than a simple identification with rational thought would suggest. In Chapter 11 we shall see how the breadth of types of interpretative response is the basis of non-human creatures' capacity to interpret signs.

The centurion's orders: interpretative actions

In this passage, the soldiers and the slave each interpret the centurion's command with an *action*. When the centurion says to those under him, "go", "come", or "do this" they go, they come, or they do it. There is no sense here of the response to the sign (the command) being mediated by a thought. Indeed, in the centurion's eyes, perhaps soldiers and slaves had best not have too many thoughts of their own. Parade-ground drill is a demonstration of a series of automatic responses to a series of signs; that is, interpretations in the form of actions.

In everyday life there are certain situations in which automatic actions are the most appropriate form of interpretation. An experienced driver will have learned to stop at red traffic lights without any deliberation, possibly while engaged in some other complex task such as conversation with their passenger. When a frog perceives something black crossing its visual field the frog's interpretation of it as a fly does not involve a thought, but consists of a rapid co-ordinated snapping action of tongue and mouth.

Actions have about them something of the character of Otherness. This is because at the simplest level of analysis an action is simply a change from one state to another state – from coming to going, from not doing to doing, from watching to snapping. Furthermore, actions impinge on the rest of the world by a brute actuality that is also the domain of Otherness. Thoughts connect things in the world and make sense of them (sometimes). Thoughts are effective; they have consequences. But they do so indirectly, often through actions. Actions, on the other hand, affect the world directly.

Interpretative actions are therefore manifestations of the elemental ground of Otherness.

◯ *Grieving for Lazarus: interpretative feelings*

In this passage, Jesus encounters Mary and the other grieving friends of her brother. He interprets the situation represented by this scene of grief not (initially) with a thought or an action, but with a *feeling*. He was "disturbed in spirit and deeply moved." The wonderfully expressive Greek word used by John is *splanchnizomai*, meaning to be moved in one's very guts.

Psychologists and neuroscientists increasingly acknowledge the cognitive role of emotions. Their ground-breaking work is helping to overturn the bias that assumes that the primary modes of cognition are rational and thought-based. Emotions are now recognized as being much more important to cognitive processes than was previously envisaged. In some ways, however, the fruitfulness of this line of inquiry simply reflects the fact that a feeling can be a kind of interpretation.

A feeling, as I suggested in the previous chapter, just *is what it is*. You can't get behind it; you can't substitute a thought or an idea in its place. Feelings have an immediacy and irreducibility, the hard-to-pin-down characteristics of 'in-itself-ness'.

Feelings, in other words, are the form of interpretation that depend on and manifest the element of Quality.

❀

What relevance does all of this have for trinitarian theology?

At risk of stating the obvious, one of the problems for trinitarian thought is to say how God can exist as three 'persons' or 'subsistences', or whatever term one chooses to use, without undermining the divine unity. In other words, is the tri-unity of God consistent with the strict monotheism that emerged within the Hebrew tradition, or do Christians really believe in three Gods rather than one?

Broadly speaking, there are two main strategies for defending the one-ness of God in a trinitarian context. The first is to base one's account of God's unity in the person of the Father, from whom the other persons in some sense derive their being. This approach inevitably brushes with subordinationism, making the Son and Spirit to some degree inferior to the Father. The problem with subordinationism is that if the Son (and/or Spirit) is less divine than the Father, the Father cannot have been fully revealed by the Son. And, if that were the case, it would not be possible for creaturely existence to be genuinely redeemed by the Incarnation of the Son/Word.[1]

The second approach is to base the unity of the 'persons' on what they share in common: some kind of divine substance or essence. The problem with this approach is that it errs towards modalism, making the Father, Son and Spirit merely three different ways in which the one divine essence may choose to appear at any particular time and place. The problem with modalism is that it would mean that the intra-trinitarian dynamic of Father, Son and Spirit, a dynamic that we infer from our own Spirit-guided encounter with the incarnate Word, is not genuine. But if this dynamic is not genuine, there is no prospect of non-divine creatures really being able to participate in the divine life.[2]

Trinitarian theology has often attempted to avoid or mitigate subordinationism and modalism by speaking of the mutual indwelling, co-inherence and dynamic interdependence of the persons within God's eternal being. This is undoubtedly a good strategy, based on a genuine insight. It is a strategy, however, that carries its own risks. One of these, it seems to me, is that it is possible to become so enamoured with terms such as 'mutual indwelling' or 'dynamic interdependence' that we allow ourselves to tolerate a serious lack of clarity about what they actually mean. I would like to suggest that the semiotic model provides a helpful way of being more specific about these terms, and therefore offers a new way of appreciating that the three-ness of God does not undermine the divine unity. This way of thinking about how the processes of signification offer a model of trinitarian indwelling may become clear if we draw together what we have just seen about the sub-divisions of the structure of signs (see diagram overleaf).

Look first at the large, pale shapes. These represent the main dimensions of the structure of signs: the 'sign-in-itself', the sign–object relation and the interpretation. As we have seen, each of these dimensions corresponds to one of the elemental grounds, which is why the large shapes are the triad of circle, square and triangle.

1 We will consider the Incarnation in the following chapter and the connection between the semiotic model and theories of atonement in Chapter 8.
2 Participation in the divine life will be the subject of Chapters 6 and 7.

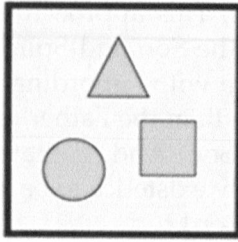

*Sign–object
relation*

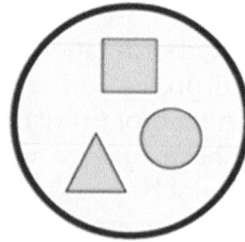

Sign-in-itself

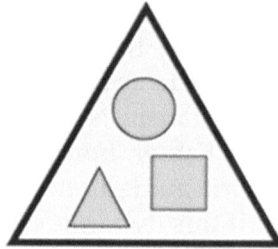

Interpretation

Now look *within* the large shapes in the diagram at their own, threefold sub-divisions. Within the sign–object relation we have icons, indexes and symbols, and each of these again corresponds to one of the elemental grounds. Therefore, within the large square (the sign–object relation) the triad of shapes corresponding to Quality, Otherness and Mediation recurs. Likewise, we have seen that there are three kinds of interpretation (feelings, actions and thoughts), each manifesting one of the elemental grounds. So within the large triangle (interpretation) the triad of circle, square, and triangle appears again.

I realize that the reader may find themselves somewhat puzzled at this point if they have spotted that, when we saw the prototype of this diagram (p. 22), the large circle was labelled as standing for either the sign or the object. Immediately after that, when I used Augustine's account to help clarify what I mean by a 'semiotic model' of the Trinity, I spoke as if it is the 'object' that corresponds to the person of the Father. In the diagram above, however, I am identifying the large circle primarily with the sign (that is, what the sign is in itself) rather than with the object. It may appear that by doing so I am attempting a sleight of hand. If earlier I associated the Father with the object, and now the object has in effect been replaced in the diagram by the sign-in-itself, with which aspect of the semiotic 'triad' am I really linking the Father? Am I presenting a solution to the problem of the divine three-ness-in-unity by surreptitiously removing the Father from the picture?!

If such questions trouble the reader (and indeed, even if they do not), now is an opportunity for me to try and make something absolutely clear about the semiotic model. The individual 'players' in any event of signification – the sign, object and interpreting agent – do not primarily correspond to the Father, Son and Holy Spirit. Rather, the interplay between the elemental grounds of Quality, Otherness and Mediation models the tri-unity of God. Both the sign and the object have an in-itself-ness about them. In the previous chapter, the in-itself-ness with which we were mostly concerned was that of the object. On the other hand, in the following discussion when we think about in-itself-ness, we will be more interested in the in-itself-ness of the sign. Both of these kinds of in-itself-ness – of the sign and that of the object – are aspects of Quality, and it is primarily the elemental ground of Quality that has resonances with the 'unbegotten-ness' of the Father. Likewise, it is not simply the sign as such that corresponds to the Word, but rather the Otherness between the sign and the object. Similarly, the Spirit is not simply the interpreter in the triad: the Spirit is properly identified as the intra-trinitarian interpreter because it is the ground of Mediation, the elemental ground upon which all interpretations depend.

Focussing, then, on the sign-in-itself, I think the fact that the diagram implies that there is, again, a threefold subdivision (the small shapes within the large circle) will not surprise you. However, I want to delay our discussion and naming of this further triad until the following chapter. For the moment, you will simply have to take it from me that the sign-in-itself does indeed divide in a threefold pattern corresponding to the three elemental grounds of signification.

A sense of what the sign-in-itself is can be gleaned from the example of a knock at a door (see box overleaf).

Now take a few moments to look again at the diagram opposite. Notice that within each of the main dimensions of signification, each represented by the shape corresponding to the relevant elemental ground, the full set of elemental grounds recurs. In other words, within each of the large shapes there is a full set of the same shapes in smaller form. Consider, then, the sense

Behold, I stand at the door and knock.

As a small boy at primary school I was once asked to take a message to the headmaster's office. Doubting that my little knuckles would produce an adequate knock on his imposing door, I decided to give it a couple of good slaps with the palm of my hand. Another teacher who was passing saw this and roundly told me off for my rudeness. Rightly so, because I had disregarded the rules for producing a sign signifying a polite request to enter a room. The unwritten rules specify that one's knuckles should be used to make the door resonate just loud enough to be reliably heard inside. Slapping or kicking the door, or even knocking more loudly, are signs produced according to different rules or conventions, with altogether different connotations.

A knock at a door is a sign-in-itself. It has an indexical relation to its object – the person doing the knocking – because the person who wishes to enter the room *causes* the knock. In the dimension of the sign–object relation the knock is therefore a manifestation of Otherness. But as a sign-in-itself it manifests Mediation since (as I learned to my cost in this incident) the knock is produced according to a rule. This rule mediates between (connects together) all other instances of this kind of sign. Indeed, it is because the sign is produced according to a mediating rule that the interpreter knows from experience that it is a sign. A knock at a door is therefore the kind of sign-in-itself represented by the small triangle within the large circle (p.40). We will look at the subdivisions of the sign-in-itself in more detail in the next chapter, where we will also see the kinds of sign-in-itself that are represented by the small circle and small square within the large circle.

Note that the rule for producing the knock at the door is in a different dimension in the structure of signs to a rule that connects a symbol to its object. This is because a symbol is a kind of sign–object relation whereas a knock at the door is an example of a sign-in-itself.

in which a characteristic of the processes of signification is that the elemental grounds fully indwell one another. None of the dimensions of signification, or their corresponding elemental grounds, exists independently of the other elemental grounds. Therefore, any event of representation and interpretation has about it a kind of unity, a unity that derives from the mutual indwelling of the three elemental grounds. Since, as we have seen, Quality, Otherness and Mediation have some kind of parallel with the Father, Son and Spirit respectively, signification offers a way of understanding how the three-ness-in-unity of God is based on the mutual indwelling of the trinitarian persons.

⚘

If signification consisted merely of a series of isolated events, the model of mutual indwelling suggested above would appear rather static and mechanical. In reality, though, sign-processes are continuous and dynamic. Indeed, semiotic theory has a rather nice term for this process: *semiosis*. To capture the nature of semiosis, we need to make the analogy more dynamic. Imagine, therefore, that we set the various shapes of our mutual-indwelling diagram into motion (p.40). We can imagine, perhaps, the whole thing rotating so that the constituent shapes, large and small, continuously tumble over and through one another. I have in mind something like the movement of the coloured glass shapes of a child's kaleidoscope, as seen when one end is held to the eye and the other slowly turned by hand.

It is this constant movement, juxtaposition and interaction of Quality, Otherness and Mediation that makes up what I have earlier referred to as the 'sea of signs'. It is a medium in constant flux: one interpretation follows another and an interpretative response to one sign will alter the kinds of sign that we will next look for and expect. Furthermore, an interpretation (thought, feeling or action) may itself become a sign to ourselves or to someone else, to be interpreted in turn by another interpretative response and so on.

Imagine that you are speaking. While doing so, you may barely be aware that you have communicated simultaneously with words, gestures and the tone of your voice. Within even the simplest of our communications there may be multiple, overlapping layers of types of sign, kinds of sign–object relation, and modes of interpretative response that we intend to elicit. This would be so even if one were delivering a monologue: a talk, a lecture or a sermon, perhaps. Think how much richer and more complex such a dynamic becomes if you are engaged in a dialogue with someone, when speaking alternates with listening and your interpretation of what you hear prompts you to respond with further facial expressions, gestures and words. Even with just two people involved it would soon become impossible to keep conscious track of the diverse signs exchanged and interpretations made.

Of course, the kaleidoscope metaphor does not replace our understanding of the mutual indwelling of the elemental grounds that is depicted statically in the diagram. Rather, it incorporates it. The kaleidoscope metaphor adds a sense of the dynamic nature of this indwelling. Indeed, the way of understanding the mutual interdependence of the trinitarian persons that has been developed in this chapter is complementary to the similar conclusion that we previously reached in Chapter 2 by analysing the overall structure of signification in the context of Augustine's approach. We noted there the mutual interdependence of Father, Son and Spirit that is implied by the fact that the Word is uttered by the Father, this utterance being dependent on, and elicited by, the Father's anticipation of the interpretation of the Word by the Spirit (p. 30).

This endless movement of the trinitarian persons with and within one another is known in trinitarian theology by the Greek word *perichoresis*. The verb *perichoreuo* means to dance around (*peri* = around; *choreia* = dance, as in choreography). The image of a dance helpfully captures the idea of the dynamic mutual interaction of the persons.[3] The semiotic model similarly draws on the dance of the elemental grounds: the perpetual kaleidoscopic movement of Quality, Otherness and Mediation (Father, Son and Spirit) in and around one another. What I am suggesting is that the dynamic indwelling of the elemental grounds that is played out in the perpetual movement of the processes of representation and interpretation bears a likeness to the eternal dynamic of the co-inherence of Father, Son and Spirit.

In short, *semiosis* models *perichoresis*.

---

3 The origins of the use of the word *perichoresis* to describe the life of the Trinity are somewhat complex. It must be admitted that it originally entered theology via the verb *perichoreo*, which means to reach around or go around and is unconnected with dancing.

4

The Colour of Love

Recently I had the pleasure of watching a team of workers painting double yellow lines along the kerb outside our house. The pleasure was not at the prospect of fewer cars being parked there (in fact the parking scheme was rather ill-conceived), but because I like seeing people making signs.

When someone is in the process of making a sign, especially if making it requires a degree of effort, they may well be concentrating on the sign-in-itself: the concretely embodied sign and how it functions as a sign. As we will see, this is a distinct, though complementary, question to that of how the sign relates to its object.

In the previous chapter I asked you to take it from me that the sign-in-itself can come in three different kinds, just as there are three kinds of sign–object relation and three kinds of interpretation. At that stage, I did not want to delay consideration of the semiotic approach to the Trinity any longer than was necessary, though we did touch briefly on the fact that one kind of sign-in-itself is produced according to a rule for its production. My example was a knock at the door, illustrated by my embarrassing childhood experience of having failed to observe the relevant rule when trying to alert the headmaster to my presence outside his office. We must now look properly at the three kinds of sign-in-itself. This final piece of the jigsaw of the structure of signs will prove to be central to my discussion of the Incarnation. Using our familiar kind of diagram, we can represent the three kinds of sign-in-itself like this:

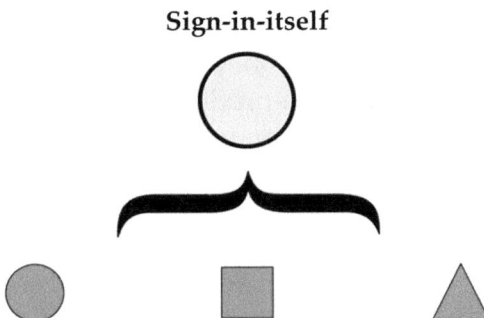

Sign-in-itself

Note that the overarching elemental ground here is Quality (the large circle, the sign in its in-itself-ness). Within the in-itself-ness of the sign we are looking for three different kinds of sign, represented by the smaller circle, square and triangle. We will name these subtypes of sign as we go along.

Let us start on the right, with the subtype represented by the triangle. This was the kind of sign-in-itself illustrated by a knock at the door. Double yellow lines are another example. In the UK, double yellow lines painted along the kerb communicate the message "no parking here." In terms of the sign–object relation, the yellow lines are a symbol because the relation between the lines and their meaning is given by a convention. However, we are concerned here with the sign-in-itself. The key point is that, as with the knock at the door, painting double yellow lines involves a rule.

Importantly, the rule for making the double yellow lines is not the same as the rule that connects the sign with the object (that is, the rule for interpreting the lines). Drivers who want to learn how to interpret the sign to avoid contravening parking regulations can look it up in the Highway Code. But the rule for *making* the sign will not be found there. Instead, I assume it would be found in some kind of Highways Agency manual which would say something like: Paint two parallel lines of such-and-such a width, separated by such-and-such a distance, using a specified type and colour of paint. And, of course, there are special road-painting machines or templates which help to ensure that the lines that are formed follow this set of rules.

Let us call this a 'rule-produced sign'. What characterizes double yellow lines or a knock at the door – in terms of the nature of their embodiment as a sign rather than their relation to their object – is that they are produced according to a rule. And notice, further, that this rule connects not the sign with the object, but this particular sign with all other instances of the same sign. Such signs are connected by the rule by which they were, or may be, produced. To use a piece of terminology from semiotic theory, they are individual 'tokens' of a general 'type'. The fact that all instances of this type of sign are *connected* by a rule means that they participate in, and depend on, the element of Mediation. Rule-produced signs therefore occupy the far right position on the diagram, represented by the triangle.

Imagine, now, a different kind of sign, again one that is sometimes seen on the road. I'm thinking of those big splatters of paint that have somehow become streaked across the carriageway. Although I've never seen it happen, I imagine that these are caused by a tin of paint accidentally falling from a builder's (or line-painter's?) lorry.

If so, these splashes on the road are not produced by a rule, they just happen. They are not deliberately formed tokens of a certain type but they can nevertheless be signs. They may be a sign, for example, of the carelessness of the person who loaded the truck. Minimally, they are a sign of a specific event having occurred; a sign that a tin of paint leaked onto the road at this particular location.

I suggest we call this kind of sign a 'stand-alone' sign. This term is appropriate because the splatter of paint would act as a sign whether or not there were ever any similar instances (though it happens that we have probably all seen many).

I have pointed out that rule-produced signs manifest the elemental ground of Mediation. It may be less easy to see that a stand-alone sign manifests Otherness. It does so because, whereas a rule-produced sign is a sign by virtue of having been formed according to a rule, a stand-alone sign is a sign merely by virtue of occurring as opposed to not occurring. Of course, in a sense this is true of rule-produced signs too: if a rule-produced sign is not there, it is not a sign. But in the case of a stand-alone sign, it is the brute actuality of the sign – its existence rather than non-existence – that constitutes it as a sign. And actuality (verses non-actuality) is a manifestation of the element of Otherness.

So, rule-produced signs manifest Mediation, and stand-alone signs manifest Otherness. The latter kind occupies the middle position on the diagram, the small square. Both kinds fall under the overarching circle (the element of Quality) of the in-itself-ness of the sign. But what sort of sign-in-itself specifically manifests the element of Quality (the circle on the left)?

Suppose that I'm looking at some yellow lines on the road, lines that are there to signify a parking prohibition. But now suppose that my interest is not in what they mean or how they were produced, but simply in their colour. My attention might become focussed specifically on their yellowness, or even on the very particular shade of yellow that they embody. I might even look at them and say to myself, that's exactly the colour I'd like to paint my house. Now, if the yellow of double yellow lines seems an unlikely colour for a house, it happens to be pretty much the colour our neighbours have painted theirs! And just supposing that our neighbours did indeed use the colour of the yellow lines to inform their choice, the yellow paint on the road would have been operating for them simply as a sign of that particular shade of yellow. In that case, the sign-in-itself would have been acting as a sign by virtue of the very quality that it embodied: it would have been a sign of nothing other than the exact quality that makes it a sign. This kind of sign is called a 'quali-sign'.

So, quali-signs are signs whose sign-hood consists in embodying a quality. It is more likely, I suspect, that our neighbours chose their paint from a sheet of colour samples in a shop than by looking at the road markings outside (the similarity with the latter presumably being accidental). If so, the colour chart was a set of quali-signs, each sample of colour being a quali-sign of a possible choice of colour for their house. Indeed, colour samples are a prime example of quali-signs. But not all quali-signs are as simple as colour samples. In order to appreciate the surprising power of quali-signs, we must think a little further about the nature of qualities.

❀

My wife is a very good cook, but she does like to play a somewhat annoying game. Having served up a delicious meal she will ask our guests, "Can you taste the secret ingredient?" Usually the answer is something like ginger, chocolate or marmite – something included in a recipe in which that particular ingredient might be rather unexpected. My frustration with this game stems from the fact that it seems to me one enjoys the taste of a special dish as a whole, not broken down into its constituent parts. Certainly some flavour or another may shine through, but the dish has a unique quality of taste in its totality, to which all the ingredients contribute. The trick of cookery, surely, is the gift of being able to make a total quality that is more than merely a mixture of the individual ingredients. In other words, we may say that qualities can be 'compound' as well as 'simple': a set of individual qualities may be combined to produce a whole that is greater than the sum of its parts. An adventurous cook may be able to create a new, perhaps previously unknown, quality.

I'd like to take this line of argument a step further and suggest that each of us embodies a unique quality of our own. One might call this total-person quality our 'personality'. Or perhaps we could call it our 'soul'. It is the sum-total of everything that we are. Of course, this is a compound quality; many ingredients make it up. But, added together, there is a wholeness to our being that has a quality all of its own. It is what is unique about us, the total quality of our personal self.

In our earlier example, the yellow colour of the road markings acted as an exemplar of a particular quality – a particular shade of yellow. We also saw that colour samples are familiar examples of quali-signs. Importantly, some qualities can only be embodied in quite particular circumstances or conditions. For example, it might be possible for a certain colour to be embodied in some kinds of fabric but not others. To obtain an exact match of colour, a very specific kind of material might be needed: dyed silk rather than dyed cotton, acrylic paint rather than watercolour. In other words, the details of the material embodiment of a quality may be essential to its having that particular quality.

Qualities, then, are sometimes very closely, even inseparably, related to the material or 'fabric' in which they are embodied. I will contend in the remainder of this chapter that these two points about qualities – that they can be 'compound' in nature and that they can sometimes only be embodied in certain substrates or circumstances – have far-reaching implications. These features of qualities, and therefore of quali-signs, will help us make some sense of traditional Christian thinking about the Incarnation.

❀

"Logic!" said the Professor half to himself. "Why don't they teach logic at these schools? There are only three possibilities. Either your sister is telling lies, or she is mad, or she is telling the truth. You know that she doesn't tell lies and it is obvious that she is not mad. For the moment then and unless any further evidence turns up, we must assume she is telling the truth."[1]

Susan and Peter have gone to see the professor because they are concerned about their sister Lucy who claims to have discovered a magical world called Narnia through the back of an old wardrobe. The professor's response – that she must be mad, bad or telling the truth – echoes an argument that C.S. Lewis, the creator of Narnia, presents elsewhere for the divinity of Jesus. Jesus claimed to be the Son of God (or, in other ways implied his equality with God). Since he was obviously neither mad nor bad, the rational response is to accept his claim and acknowledge his divinity.[2]

Much as I admire C.S. Lewis, there are, of course, problems with this argument. To begin with, do 'mad', 'bad' or 'telling the truth' really exhaust the possibilities? And even if Jesus did explicitly claim to be the Son of God (which is far from certain), what would this turn of phrase have meant to him and his listeners? Biblical scholars tell us that 'Son of God' would commonly have been used to refer to someone who had been specially appointed as God's servant, such as a king. Moreover, since the New Testament contains no clearly

1 C.S. Lewis, *The Lion, the Witch and the Wardrobe*. (London: Geoffrey Bles, 1950), pp. 49-50.
2 C.S. Lewis, *Mere Christianity*. (London: Fontana, 1955, first published 1952), pp. 51-53.

formulated doctrine of the Trinity, it doesn't make sense to read 'Son of God' in this context as a claim that Jesus was the second person of the Trinity.

One standard way of dealing with these sorts of objection is to hold that Jesus, in his human life, had no specific, personal knowledge of being divine. Rather, the recognition of his divinity came to others later on as a result of reflection on his life, death and resurrection. Only then, it is argued, did it begin to be coherent to speak of Jesus as God's unique Son in the sense of the Incarnation of the eternal Word. That, I suppose, is the kind of view that I vaguely accepted for a long time. I was shaken out of it by reading N.T. Wright's essay, 'Jesus' Self-understanding.'[3]

Wright rejects the idea that we have no way of knowing whether Jesus understood himself to be related in a special way to Israel's God, YHWH. What we know of Jesus' ministry, he suggests, makes perfect sense in the context of the hopes and expectations of first century Jews. Briefly, Wright's idea is that Jesus understood his own life as being an embodiment of YHWH's decisive return to Jerusalem. Although Israel's exile in Babylon had ended some five centuries earlier, this had not amounted to the ultimate fulfilment of God's promised Kingdom. After the Babylonian exile the Temple had been rebuilt in Jerusalem, but the building awaited the arrival of its rightful inhabitant. According to the Judaism of this Second Temple period, YHWH's eventual triumphant return to the city would herald the defeat of the nation's enemies and its deliverance from evil. God would again occupy the Temple, reign over his people, and draw all the nations of the earth into his glorious Kingdom.

Wright suggests that Jesus understood his ministry as an 'enacted parable' of YHWH's return to Jerusalem and of his (God's) victory over the powers of evil. This enactment was not, however, a simple fulfilment of the expectation of Second Temple Judaism. Rather, the mode of kingly reign that Jesus enacted during his journey(s) towards and final entry into Jerusalem were a deliberate subversion of first-century Jewish expectations. The Jewish people expected YHWH to overthrow the Roman occupiers. Jesus, in contrast, opposed violent responses to the Roman occupation, believing that the ultimate enemy, the dark power behind Israel's suffering, was not Rome but Satan. Jesus' call for an abandonment of violent nationalistic aspirations was likewise accompanied by a re-working of the key elements of Jewish belief. The expectation of restored land became, in Jesus' enactment

3 N.T. Wright, 'Jesus' Self-understanding,' in *The Incarnation*, edited by Stephen T. Davies, Daniel Kendall and Gerald O'Collins (Oxford: Oxford University Press, 2002), pp. 47-61.

of the arrival of YHWH's Kingdom, a drama of restored human lives and communities. The traditional Jewish emphasis on the family was redefined in Jesus' ministry by his controversial fellowship with sinners. The Torah was to find its fulfilment in the kind of life to be lived by those who had themselves been recipients of the mercy and forgiveness enacted in Jesus' ministry.

Jesus' embodiment of YHWH's definitive return to Jerusalem took the form, then, of an 'enacted parable'. As Wright puts it, Jesus intended to "enact, symbolize and personify" God's return to his rightful dwelling place.[4] Jesus' whole ministry was directed towards and constituted this enactment, moving towards its climax in his entry into Jerusalem. Within the culminating scenes of this enacted parable stand a pair of crucial acts of signification: his action in the Temple and the Last Supper. Wright refers to these as 'symbolic' actions, but this non-technical use of the term 'symbol' does not precisely capture the type of sign that is involved. In semiotic terms, I suggest that Wright's thesis implies that in his entire ministry Jesus was deliberately forming his life into an *icon*, an image of God's presence in the world. And, as we shall see, both of the climactic acts of signification in the last week of Jesus' life, the Temple action and the Last Supper, were iconic in nature.

The question is, if Jesus' life was an embodied enactment of YHWH's presence in the world, does the semiotic model help us to understand what Christian theology means when it speaks of the Incarnation – what it means to say that Jesus was the Word made flesh? Thinking about the different ways in which the Temple action and the Last Supper were iconic signs may give us a clue.

❦

In the Synoptic Gospels, soon after Jesus goes up to Jerusalem for his last Passover, he finds traders and money changers working in the Temple. His angry response is to drive out the traders and their animals with a whip of cords and to overturn the tables of the money changers. In John's Gospel, bystanders ask him, "What sign can you show us for doing this?" to which Jesus makes an enigmatic reply about the destruction of the Temple and his raising it up in three days (John 2: 19).

It is well known that John's Gospel makes frequent references to Jesus' signs. The turning of water into wine at the wedding at Cana is described as "the first of his signs" (John 2: 11), and in John's Gospel the Temple action follows within a few days of this (2: 13-22). Unlike

4 N.T. Wright, *Jesus and the Victory of God* (London: SPCK, 1996), p. 615.

the synoptics, then, John does not place the Temple action within the final days of Jesus' life. Instead, John's version of the event occurs near the beginning of what some have called John's 'book of signs'. Whenever it actually occurred, John's context invites us to ask, what kind of sign was Jesus' action in the Temple?

We have just seen that Wright refers to the Temple action loosely as a 'symbol'. But, as I have indicated, according to the more formal semiotic terminology with which we have been working, the Temple action was not a symbol but an icon. Why? Because the drama that unfolded that day in the Temple was a sign that was related to its object by a kind of resemblance. Specifically, Jesus' outburst signified a judgement on the Temple and, indeed, a prediction of its future destruction. Overturning the money changers' tables would have caused a temporary interruption to the normal running of the Temple system. As such it was an iconic representation – a brief but striking likeness – of the permanent disruption that would occur were the Temple to be destroyed, whether functionally, by way of decisive divine judgement, or literally, as occurred in AD 70.

To say that the Temple action was an icon is to identify the kind of sign–object relation that was involved. However, if the sign was an icon (rather than an index or symbol) of the judgement that it represented, what should we say about it as a sign-in-itself? In other words, was it a rule-produced sign, a stand-alone sign, or a quali-sign?

We can say first that the Temple action was not a sign produced or reproduced according to a rule for its production. Jesus did not make a habit of making a scene in the Temple, and did not instruct his disciples to do likewise. Nor was it a sign that signified purely by embodying a quality, though obviously there were various qualities in play in the drama. We may conclude, at the level of signification concerned with the sign-in-itself, that the Temple action was a stand-alone sign: it signified simply by being an event that occurred. The basis of its sign-hood, what allowed it to stand as a sign, was simply that it happened (as opposed to not having happened). In short, Jesus' Temple action was an *iconic stand-alone* sign of judgement on the religious order of his day.

The second of the crucial acts of signification picked out by Wright as central to Jesus' enactment of YHWH's presence is the Last Supper. Like the Temple action, the Last Supper was an iconic sign. It represented its object by a kind of likeness. It recalled Jesus' inclusive 'table fellowship', his controversial practice of eating with sinners and outcasts that had been so central to his ministry, and it anticipated the eschatological banquet that, in Hebrew tradition, was an important way of envisioning the future Kingdom of God.

But the Last Supper was not a stand-alone event. Jesus instructed that the sign which it constituted should be repeated by his disciples. The Last Supper was the exemplar of a type of sign that was to be repeatedly reproduced in the form of tokens of that type. Jesus set the pattern for these future eucharistic instantiations of the sign as he took, gave thanks, broke and shared the bread, saying, "Do this in remembrance of me" (Luke 22: 19). Paul later added some don'ts to the rules (1 Corinthians 11: 17-34). The Eucharist – based on the Last Supper as its template – is therefore an *iconic rule-produced sign.*

⚛

The Temple action and the Last Supper, the two great signs of the coming Kingdom that Jesus enacted in Jerusalem in the days before his death, were therefore two different kinds of iconic sign. One was an iconic stand-alone sign, the other an iconic rule-produced sign.[5]

Let us now recall the earlier part of this chapter, in which I suggested that a whole human life could have a particular and unique total quality of its own. Just as all the individual ingredients of a dish combine to produce a total quality of taste, so all the ingredients of a life can combine to produce a total quality of lived existence. This was true of Jesus' life, just as it is true of yours and mine. Our discussion about the Temple action and the Last Supper as two types of iconic sign now suggests a way of speaking about the whole of Jesus' life and ministry as a certain kind of sign. We have seen that it is possible to think of the totality of Jesus' life as being the embodiment of the very being and presence of YHWH. Indeed, Wright's contention is that this is exactly how Jesus understood his life and actions. Earlier in the chapter we saw that there is a kind of sign-in-itself whose capacity to act as a sign lies in the very quality that it embodies. We may say, then, that the totality of Jesus' life and death was a *quali-sign* of God the Father. Taken as a whole, the sum of everything that Jesus did and said embodied, in human form, the exact quality of God's transforming love. In relation to what it represented, namely God the Father, Jesus' life and death signified by a kind of resemblance or likeness, so it was an icon. As a sign-in-itself, Jesus' life-and-death embodied a particular total quality: it was a quali-sign. In short, the sum-total of Jesus' life and death was an *iconic quali-sign* of God the Father.

Of course, it would be absurd to suggest that Jesus had all of this

---

5 As an aside, I sometimes wonder what it would be like if Jesus had instituted these signs the other way round. Wouldn't it be liberating if the climax of church worship involved a cathartic overturning of the furniture!

specifically in mind when he rode a donkey into Jerusalem, or caused a disturbance in the Temple, or gave his disciples instructions to prepare a final Passover meal. I am not suggesting that any philosophical theory of signs lay consciously behind any of these actions, or that he was systematically working through the available subtypes of sign. But if Jesus' intention was to enact and embody YHWH's definitive return to Jerusalem, it is not surprising to find that his life involved a series of acts of iconic signification. Moreover, if he intended these various iconic enactments to add up to a unified whole, it should not come as a surprise that the individual acts of signification turn out to have covered the whole range of types of iconic representation.

Jesus was not unusual in the fact that the total fabric of his life consisted of a tapestry of individual acts of signification. We are all continuously engaged in a process of forming ourselves into signs. Whenever we choose what to wear, how to speak, how to act, we are constructing signs that say something about us. The process of constructing these signs is part of what makes us who we are. Even if we try to avoid signifying anything by our appearance or behaviour, that avoidance itself becomes a sign of something.

We humans have always made ourselves and our possessions into vehicles for signification. Whether by painting our bodies with ochre and decorating them with strings of pierced shells, or by dressing in a certain way and socializing with certain groups of people, we are constantly (and unconsciously) making ourselves into signs.

For humans – and in this Jesus was the same as the rest of us – it is not a question of whether to make ourselves into signs, but of what signs to make.

※

The Temple action, the Last Supper, and Jesus' whole life and ministry contain all three possible permutations of iconic sign: iconic stand-alone signs, iconic rule-produced signs and, overall, an iconic quali-sign. "So what?", you may ask. Why would it be of any interest to think about Jesus' life and death as being a quali-sign of God's eternal nature?

One answer is that the semiotic perspective helps because it sets historical work such as that of Wright within a wider conceptual context. That context – the theory of signs – has the potential to make connections with other areas of theological, philosophical and scientific thought.[6] Indeed, this whole book may be regarded as

---

6 Wright himself asks how his historical thesis might provide a context within which to rethink some of the traditional debates within systematic theology: see 'Jesus's Self-understanding', pp. 55-56.

an attempt to show that a new kind of coherence begins to emerge when the traditional theological landscape is viewed in the light of semiotic theory.

For the moment, let us focus on a specific way in which thinking about the Incarnation in semiotic terms is helpful. For the theory of signs to be useful, it must help solve a problem. What is the biggest problem with Christian thinking about the Incarnation? I put it to you that a major difficulty arises when we attempt to affirm that Jesus was fully, totally and unreservedly human. In other words, given that the Christian tradition holds that Jesus was fully divine, the difficulty is in holding, alongside this claim, the parallel conviction that Jesus was as human as you or me. The perpetual temptation is to see Jesus as being in some way less than fully human. Instead of affirming that the fullness of God's being was expressed in the wholeness of a human person, we come to think of God having walked around on earth disguised as a man.

If we succumb to this temptation, we will be led to speak in ways that imply that the humanity of Jesus was primarily an appearance rather than a fact, that there was something about Jesus that was not really human in the same way as other humans. This way of thinking goes by the name of docetism, a tendency of thought that the church officially rejects as unorthodox – that is, inconsistent with the overall message of the New Testament. I suspect, though, that docetism in one form or another is the default position of many Christians. The ultimate problem with such a view is that if Jesus was not fully human – as human as you or me – it is difficult to see how his life can offer salvation to actual, everyday, flesh-and-blood humans.

When we were teenagers, my sister and I repeatedly pestered our parents to upgrade their Ford Cortina to a Volvo Estate. Unfortunately, for whatever reason, they went in the other direction and downgraded to a 1970s-brown Morris Marina. The wound to my adolescent self-image was only healed when, as a father of teenage children myself, I bought a Volvo for our own family. The justification for the initial outlay has, so far, proved to be warranted: the car has gone twice 'round the clock' and still drives like the day we bought it. However, if you looked under the bonnet you would see that the car is not fully a Volvo. Behind its performance and reliability, underneath its characteristic Swedish lines, there is a rather fine Audi engine.

Many of our difficulties in talking about Jesus as both fully human and fully divine arise when we think about humans as having certain parts that can be taken by non-human replacements. In other words, the thing that most predisposes to a docetic view of Jesus' divinity is a dualistic view of our own humanity. Dualism is the view that human existence (or the world in general) is divided into two distinct realms. On the one hand we think of material things, things composed of matter. We contrast matter with what we think of as non-material things like mind, soul or spirit. If we think of human beings in this way, it is easy to think of Jesus as having possessed the human elements of the material realm and divine elements of the spiritual realm. But if that was the case then Jesus was not fully human.

This heresy is called Apollinarianism, a fourth-century version of docetism. Apollinaris held that the Incarnation came about as a result of the eternal divine Word taking the place of Jesus' human mind or soul. According to that view Jesus would be like my car – Swedish in appearance but German under the bonnet; human in outward respects, but divine where (according to this way of thinking) it really matters.

My account of the person of Jesus as an iconic quali-sign of the Father gives us a different way of thinking about the Incarnation (and perhaps also of the resurrection: see box overleaf). Recall the analogy that I used earlier (pp. 48-49), of the colour of a piece of fabric. Suppose that a particular quality of colour can only be fully realized within a fabric of a particular kind. According to the quali-sign view of the Incarnation, we would say that the quality of God required a certain kind of fabric in which to be embodied. The particular kind of fabric that was necessary is provided, I suggest, by the fabric of the world. Indeed, humanity in particular – the total fabric of human biological, psychological and social existence – is exactly the kind of fabric in which the quality of God can dwell.

There are at least two different ways in which the analogy of the colour of a particular material could be elaborated, consideration of which may be instructive in our thinking about the Incarnation. One version of the analogy would assert that the fabric of the world is like a piece of cloth that can be dyed. On this version, the Incarnation occurred when the fabric of the world was dyed with the 'colour' of God. In that case, the indwelling of the world by the quality of God would be rather like the indwelling of my Volvo with the power of an Audi engine. Such an account implies a dualistic view of the human person that is not easy to reconcile with current scientific accounts of humanity. Neither, for that matter, does it fit well with Hebrew insights into the psychosomatic unity of human persons.

A more satisfactory version of the analogy, therefore, would involve a colour that is intrinsic to a certain kind of fabric or material. Think, for example, of the colour of ebony – the rich, dark, almost black quality of ebony wood. The colour is intrinsic to the wood of certain species

Resurrection

I wonder whether the resurrection appearances of Jesus may be thought of as the earthly appearance of exactly what we have been discussing here – the total quality of Jesus' life, his personal being and history. This is what distinguishes resurrection from resuscitation. Resuscitation is the reappearance of a dead person who is restored to life in the same mode as before they died. The resurrection was different. It was the appearance of the sum-total quality of Jesus' personhood. While resuscitation is a reversal of dying, taking the death part (temporarily) out of a person's life-story, the resurrected Jesus incorporates the ingredient of Jesus' death into the total quality of his being. The resurrection incorporates the entire timeline of his life into a single whole. This is, I think, the reason Jesus was initially unrecognizable to some of those to whom he appeared.

This view of the resurrection fits well with something that is implied by the quali-sign account of the Incarnation; that certain qualities can be embodied in very different 'materials' and yet remain the same quality. That, of course, is exactly Paul's point in his famous passage on the resurrection: "What is sown is perishable, what is raised is imperishable . . . . It is sown a physical body, it is raised a spiritual body" (1 Corinthians 15: 42-44). In the case of Jesus' life, in a way that we cannot fully understand, Jesus' 'spiritual body' (the total summation of his life in the form of a quali-sign of his whole being) became known within the ordinary structures of space and time in the resurrection appearances.

This concept helps us to see the point of accounts of the ascension, which are a recognition that this timeless spiritual body really belongs to the realm of the eternal life of the Trinity. And of course, since the quality of Jesus' life is to be understood as a perfect representation of the being of the Father, the ascended quali-sign that is Jesus' risen body is precisely the eternal Word who has belonged with God from the beginning.

of tree – it emerges through the normal growth of the wood. Indeed, it is so distinctive that the wood gives its name to ebony as a colour. The colour has not been added to the wood from outside. Rather, that particular kind of very dense wood has, by virtue of its own structure and composition, this very specific and recognizable quality.

On this version of the analogy we could say that the fabric of the world, the world-stuff, is capable of developing in such a way that it acquires the very particular character of the quality ('colour') of

God. It is not that world-stuff and God-stuff are somehow fused together; it is that the fabric of the world can, under certain very special circumstances, take on the very quality of God. Jesus, on this account, was world-stuff formed in such a way as to be a true embodiment of the divine 'colour'. When Philip says to Jesus, "Lord, show us the Father," Jesus replies, "Whoever has seen me has seen the Father" (John 14: 9). In other words, the totality of Jesus' being has a certain quality, and that quality is the exact quality of God (the Father).

One consequence of this way of thinking is that the whole nature of the problem of understanding the Incarnation is turned around. We tend to assume that we know roughly what we mean by God and roughly what we mean by human. On this view, the puzzle of the Incarnation seems to be a question of how God could have become human. How can God-stuff dwell within human-stuff? How can they be joined together? The quali-sign approach to the Incarnation invites a paradigm shift, a completely new way of asking the question. The mystery is no longer, "How did God-stuff fuse with human stuff?" The mystery is how to look at the world and see it as a fabric capable of embodying the very quality of God. This may require us to see the world from an entirely new perspective. World-stuff has to be formed in a very particular way if it is to embody the quality of God's being. But there is no world-stuff, no ordinary matter, nothing in the universe that could not in the right circumstances bear that quality.

It is sometimes said that if we believe in the Incarnation we must recognize the essential goodness of matter. If matter has the capacity to be the bearer of the divine then it must be good. That might be said even of our fabric-and-dye version of the analogy. I would go further, however. Matter is not good merely because it can be infused with the colour of God; it is good because it can *be* the colour of God. The goodness of creation is not the goodness of silk, capable of soaking up a certain bright colour and displaying it to full advantage. The goodness of creation is the goodness of ebony, whose potential for embodying certain qualities arises from the depths of its own being. In human beings, matter has developed into precisely the form, the exact kind of 'fabric' that can embody a very particular kind of quality: namely, the very quality of God. "God is love." In Jesus, the love that God is was fully and perfectly embodied as part of the fabric of the world.

5

Three Kinds of Relation

Think back, if you will, to the discussion in Chapter 3 about the dynamic mutual indwelling of the trinitarian persons. I suggested there that the processes of signification help one reflect on the dynamic inner life of the being of God. In short, I suggested that semiosis models *perichoresis*.

Suppose, for the sake of argument, that this is indeed a good way of thinking about God's inner life – perhaps even one of the best! How much would have been achieved? The answer, sadly, is very little. Why? Because providing some kind of account of the inner being of God does not immediately reveal anything about the essence of Christian life and faith. There are two pressing issues for trinitarian theology today: first, questions about what speaking about God as Trinity has to do with the way in which God is revealed in the person of Jesus of Nazareth, and second, about how trinitarian thought may relate to the everyday practical problems of Christian discipleship. To put it in the technical language of trinitarian theology, these are questions about the relation between the immanent Trinity (the Trinity in itself) and the economic Trinity (the Trinity at work in the world).

Arguably, the reason trinitarian theology has become almost irrelevant to most Christians is that for many centuries, perhaps even for most of the history of Christian thinking, attention has tended to focus on questions about the Trinity 'in itself'. It has been assumed that questions about the immanent Trinity can be disconnected from reflection on the significance of a flesh-and-blood, first-century Palestinian Jew, and from the outworking of his life in the lives of ordinary people seeking to be his disciples.

Those familiar with these problems may already feel that, having spent much of Part I of the book talking about the immanent Trinity, I have fallen into exactly this trap. In my defence, I submit that that is a risk I had to take in order to put together a *prima facie* case for consideration of a semiotic model of the Trinity. I have tried to ameliorate the effect of setting things out in this order by introducing, as early as I reasonably could, my semiotic approach to the Incarnation. In some ways the semiotic model of the Trinity begins with consideration of the Incarnation. In other words, the starting point for trinitarian thinking (including the semiotic model) is the question, "What must be true of God *if it is the case* that God's being was fully and perfectly embodied in the person of Jesus?" In that sense my approach does, after all, start with the economic Trinity – the Trinity as revealed and experienced in the world – even if we had to work through some chapters on the immanent Trinity for that to become apparent.

In Part II of this book, we will be ready to undertake the task of thinking further about the economic Trinity by making connections between the semiotic model and the practical life of the church. Here I will be able to get to the heart of what I want to say. But first I invite you to reflect on the immanent Trinity for one further short chapter. Specifically, I want to consider how the semiotic model of the Trinity compares with the two traditional trinitarian models: the psychological and social models of the three-ness of God. If this proves to be hard going, or if you have simply had enough of thinking about God's 'inner' being, please feel free to skip ahead to Part II, 'Sharing God's Life'.

❀

Psychological analogies for the Trinity take the working of the mind as a model for the intra-trinitarian relations. The analogies identify a triad of elements of cognition which, taken together, are essential to the proper functioning of the mind. Such a triad can then be used as a way of understanding how the three persons of the Trinity relate to one another within the being of God.

Augustine, as we have seen, picked out (among others) the triad of memory, understanding and will as a possible likeness of the Trinity. Each of the elements of this triad (he supposed) has a distinct function and a specific kind of relation to the others: the mind cannot operate without all three elements interacting in harmony. He held, therefore, that the roles of memory, understanding and will within the mind offer a way of understanding how the Father, Son and Spirit are distinct but inseparable within the life of the Trinity.

The strength of psychological analogies, and not just those proposed by Augustine, is that they can illustrate how three different and distinct elements can be necessary to the operation of a unified whole. The whole would lack its wholeness, its unity, if any one of its three elements were not intrinsically related to the others. The core problem with psychological analogies, however, tends to be in their implications about human minds. If God is understood to be a perfect and self-sufficient unity, the indirect implication of the psychological analogies is that the human mind is, likewise, an autonomous, isolated entity. I doubt whether it is fair to lay the blame for such a view at Augustine's door, but it is certainly a view of the mind that has flourished from around the time of the Enlightenment onwards. It is a view that has been called into question in recent years with the recognition that human knowledge – and, indeed, human existence – is profoundly relational and communal. Psychological analogies for the Trinity are now almost inevitably tainted by their easy association with the Enlightenment picture of humans as isolated, autonomous subjects.

At the opposite pole of trinitarian thought, therefore, are social models of the Trinity which, for just this reason, have enjoyed a recent period of popularity. Social models of the Trinity take the inherently relational nature of human persons as a model for the relations between the persons of the Trinity. The strength of the social analogy is its emphasis on relationality and its consequent affirmation of relationship as the proper basis of human society. However, like the psychological approach, social models of the Trinity also have their problems. A key shortcoming of the social analogy is that it has difficulty in showing how the persons of the Trinity – Father, Son and Holy Spirit – are irreducibly distinct from one another. Three human persons in relationship with one another are three separate entities of the same basic kind. If the persons of the Trinity are the same as one another in the way that three human persons are, it is difficult to avoid the suspicion that there are in fact three Gods, not one indivisible unity. A related problem is that it is not clear in social models of the Trinity why the number of trinitarian persons should be limited to three. Why could there not be four or five persons in the eternal divine society? Wouldn't it be a case of the more, the merrier?

❀

The semiotic model combines the advantages of the psychological and social models, while avoiding the problematic aspects of both. As in the psychological analogies, the semiotic approach emphasizes that the elements of Quality, Otherness and Mediation are irreducibly distinct from one another. They are not three things of the same basic kind. Indeed, as we have seen in Chapter 2, even calling them by the same generic name (elemental grounds) is problematic. No act of representation can ever really grasp the fundamental ground of its own operation, just as musicians cannot offer definitions (as opposed to examples) of the fundamental elements of music simply by playing their instruments. And yet, in spite of this irreducible distinctiveness, and the associated impossibility of complete definition, the elemental grounds together produce a unified and inseparable whole: namely, the triadic structure of signification.

In its ability to articulate something of the irreducible distinctiveness of the trinitarian persons, the semiotic model is similar to the psychological model. However, the semiotic model gives a sense of unity-in-distinctiveness while (like the social analogies) avoiding a view of the human mind as an isolated autonomous entity. We know that human personhood emerges through our capacity to respond to *external* signs. We are continually formed and transformed by our interpretative responses to the outside world, by our interpretative feelings, thoughts and actions. The very first signs we respond to are social in nature. From our first moments, we engage with the touches, smiles and smells of our mother and first carers; signs that we are loved and are lovable. Very soon we learn to reciprocate those signs. Our capacity for imitation is evident remarkably soon after birth and neuroscience has recently uncovered some of the intriguing neuronal mechanisms of this capacity. In adult life, the range of reciprocal forms of signification and interpretation between human persons multiplies exponentially, but the basis of those interactions remains rooted in the fundamental structure of signs that we have been exploring.

In short, human sign-use is an inherently social process: making and interpreting signs is what forms us into who we are. We may rightly say, then, that human personhood is inherently relational because what makes us persons is the way in which we interact with one another using signs. We would also want to say that the being of the three trinitarian 'persons' is relational because, as we have seen, their individual being cannot be understood apart from their relations with one another. But it would be an error of logic to say that, because human persons and trinitarian 'persons' are both relational entities, trinitarian persons and human persons are directly like one another.

The connection between human relationality and trinitarian relationality is subtle. Human relationality derives from trinitarian relationality because human relationships depend on the processes of semiosis, on making and interpreting signs. All of our interactions with one another, from our earliest experiences as babies to our most complex adult exchanges of thoughts and ideas, depend on our capacity for representation and interpretation. These diverse kinds of semiosis (which, even if they are occurring within our individual minds, nevertheless depend ultimately on social forms of interaction) model the relational life, the *perichoresis*, of the persons of the Trinity. The self-sufficient semiotic life of the Trinity is modelled by the inherently social semiotic life of humans. The Trinity is not 'social' in the sense of consisting of a collection of persons like a human society. The Trinity is relational in the sense that the Father, Son and Spirit are the relational grounds of the processes of representation and interpretation.

Quite early on in my thinking about the semiotic model of the Trinity, an eminent theologian expressed the concern that he had been preaching for decades on social trinitarianism as the basis of human relationality and that my approach would require him to rewrite his standard sermon on the subject. For the reasons sketched above, I do not think that abandoning an essentially relational understanding of the Trinity and humanity is a necessary consequence of the semiotic model: the inherently relational nature of human existence is fully affirmed, and indeed underwritten, by the semiotic perspective. In fact (paradoxically, given the social trinitarians' emphasis on relationality) I believe there is a major problem with the social model's account of relations. The danger is that 'relation' may be taken to be some kind of fundamental aspect of existence, which the three trinitarian persons exemplify in their relatedness. But if that is the case, then 'relations' and 'relationality' seem to have an existence outside or prior to the being of God. And if that is so, then God's absolute sovereignty over all things is undermined because there is something (relationality) to which God is subject, something outside God which constrains or determines the nature of God's being. From a theological point of view, this won't do: relationality (and any other category or aspect of existence) must surely originate within – must have as its ultimate and only source – the being of God.

The semiotic model offers a solution to this problem because it does not rest on some general concept of relation or relationality. Rather, it suggests that there is not just one kind of relation: there are three. The elemental grounds *are* relations. Quality is the relation of in-its-selfness.[1] Otherness is the relation of difference or distinctiveness between two things. Mediation is the relation that connects otherwise distinct things. These three kinds of relation arise from – indeed they are – the three persons of the Trinity.

---

1 In some ways this may look more like absence of relation than relation, but it is a relation in the sense that its nature only makes sense in the context of the other kinds of relation, which it is not. One way of putting this is to say that Quality is a zero-order relation.

In the thirteenth century, St Thomas Aquinas spoke of the trinitarian persons as 'subsistent relations'. In other words, the persons are not entities that are in relation; they *are* the relations. The semiotic model coheres with Thomas' insight.

❀

Before we arrive at Part II of this book, let me say one more thing about the 'dance of meaning' that is the Trinity. In philosophy there is a major distinction between 'ontology', which is the study of *what there is,* and epistemology, which is the study of *how we know anything*. Central to Christian thought are, likewise, questions on the one hand about what *is* truly the case about God and the world, and on the other about how we *know* they are the case.

For it to be possible to know the truth about the world, there must be some kind of connection between what we know about the world and the way we are able to know it. The scientist–theologian John Polkinghorne used to wear a T-shirt bearing the slogan "epistemology models ontology." From a theological point of view, if this is true – if there is an ultimate coherence between being and knowledge – then the source of this coherence must be within the nature of God. For, if there were some principle of being or some mode or method of knowledge that did not arise within the very being of God, God's sovereignty would be undermined.

In the semiotic model, the origin of the coherence of being and knowledge within the triune God makes perfect sense. All knowledge rests on a capacity for representation and interpretation. We cannot say anything without using signs, and we cannot know anything without interpreting them. If signs were merely human constructs, there would be no guarantee that our capacities for representation and interpretation could ever lead us into any kind of true knowledge of the way things are – either with the world or with God. But, according to the semiotic model, God's very being is intrinsically *representational* and *interpretative*. In other words, within the very nature of God, being and knowing are one and the same thing. God is not God without being the one who utters and who interprets – the one whose own reality is an eternal signifying and knowing of that very reality. In our own everyday ways of knowing things, every time our understanding of the world coincides with the truth, or comes a step closer to coinciding with it, we imperfectly model this perfect coherence of representation-and-being that inheres within the Trinity.

Part II

Sharing God's Life

6

Partakers of the Divine Nature

Like many people of about my age – people who were children at the time when space travel became a reality – I find that the Apollo missions hold an enduring fascination. The aim of the Apollo programme was to put a man on the moon. On my shelves I have a book that explains in some detail how the various engineering challenges of this undertaking were met. It is quite a technical book and apart from a few general statements in the introduction there is very little explicit reference to the overall goal of the project. It is taken for granted, for example, that when reading about the finer points of Apollo's navigation systems the reader knows that the overall context is the problem of how to get from the earth to the moon.

I sometimes wonder whether something similar may be true of the witness of the Judaeo-Christian Scriptures. When it comes to working out the overall goal to which these Scriptures point, is it possible that we sometimes fail to see the wood for the trees? Might we sometimes mistake a sub-component of the narrative for its overall purpose? What, indeed, is the ultimate objective towards which the New Testament witness is drawing us, the earth-to-the-moon factor in Christian discipleship? Perhaps it is to bring us to confess that Jesus is the incarnate Word, the eternal Son of God? Maybe it is to enable us to receive redeeming grace through Jesus' life, death and resurrection? Or perhaps it is simply to know – and to live out the consequences of knowing – that "God is Love"?

All of these, I agree, are part of the good news. But I suspect that they are not the main event. They may be aspects of what is needed for the fulfilment of God's ultimate purposes, but I wonder whether in Scripture, as in a technical account of the Apollo missions, these purposes might be referred to only obliquely. Not, of course, because the overall goal is deliberately concealed, but because it is simply taken for granted. If so, I suggest that a candidate for this understated earth-to-the-moon factor in the Christian worldview might be this: that we are called to become "partakers of the divine nature" (2 Peter 1: 4, King James Version).

One reason why the idea of participation in the divine nature has been relatively neglected, especially in Western Christianity, may be simply that it is so astonishing. To see why it is so radical we might want to make a distinction between two different kinds of participation. Let us call these 'weak' and 'strong' participation. If I draw a circle, it will share with other circles the property of circularity. In that sense it 'participates' in circularity. One way of understanding how we could participate in God would be similar. By God's grace, we might say, we are made in a way that mirrors God's being. And by being an 'image' of God we could be said to participate in God's own nature.

That would be participation in a weak form. Now, consider a stronger version. A little while ago I became interested in jazz music. I started listening to jazz records and learning about the extraordinary lives of the jazz greats, such as Louis Armstrong, Ella Fitzgerald and Charlie Parker. As my appreciation of the music grew, I felt I had to find out whether I would be capable of playing the saxophone, so I bought an instrument and began having some lessons. Some time later I was persuaded to join a wind-band to which I now make what I hope is a useful (though not virtuosic) contribution on tenor sax. Each of these stages of my interest in jazz represent, to some degree, 'participating' in jazz. But playing in a band is, I think you would agree, a stronger form of participation than practising with a pre-recorded backing track, and each of these is a stronger form of participation than putting my precious vinyl on the turntable (joyous though that form of participation may be).

Now the question of *theosis*, to use the technical term for participation in the divine life, is not, I think, an abstract question of how we participate in the divine nature in the weak sense. Rather, it is a concrete question of how we enter the divine life in the strong sense. The Christian concept of *theosis* is not of participation in the way that a circle 'participates' in circularity or an audience 'participates' in jazz by attending a gig. It is more a matter of being drawn into the very life of God, just as I have been graciously incorporated into the musical life of a band.

This immediately means that the idea of *theosis*, of participation in God's life, must raise questions about the church. What is the church? What are the sacraments? How, if at all, does the sacramental life of the church draw us into the life of God? Moreover, what is the connection between Jesus being the incarnate Word of the Father and the hope that we, and all creatures, may have an eternal share in the being of God? How, in other words, do we get from Incarnation to *theosis*?

We can begin to answer these questions by recalling that, according to the semiotic model, the inner life of the Trinity may be thought of (as far as the inner life of God can be understood at all) as the eternal interpretation of the Word by the Spirit. The Word, which became incarnate in the person of Jesus, is the full and perfect representation (sign) of the Father. And this sign is made living and active by the power of the Spirit, who is the ground of all mediation, the one who enables the Word to be interpreted as a sign of the Father. What is eternally represented by the Word and interpreted by the Spirit is the very quality of the being of God. Through the Word and by the power of the Spirit, God is known to God's-self. This, then, is the eternal life of the Trinity: the Spirit's eternal interpretation of the Word as a perfect sign of the Father.

Participation in the divine life, in the strong sense of *theosis*, is not just a question of knowing something *about* God. It is an involvement in, an incorporation into, the very process of God's self-knowledge. If we were merely talking about a weak form of participation we might be looking at a simple mirroring of this process in the processes of human knowing. The strong version of participation in God implies much more than this. Strong participation in the divine life, fully fledged *theosis*, involves adopting, or rather being adopted into, the place held by one (or more) of the persons of the Trinity within the process of God's self-knowing.

Consider first how we might adopt, or be adopted into, the role of the Spirit. We will truly participate in the divine life if we rightly interpret the Word as the perfect representation of the Father. In that case, we are being allowed to do exactly what the Spirit normally does. Within the eternal life of the Trinity the Spirit's role is that of perpetual interpretation of the Word. But we finite temporal creatures have likewise been granted the capacity – and the opportunity – to interpret the Word as a sign of the Father. In doing so we participate in the divine life just as the Spirit does.

Importantly, such interpretation of the Word as a sign of the Father is not just an exercise of the intellect. As we saw in Chapter 3, interpretation is not merely a matter of thoughts, but also of feelings and actions. We may not employ all of these modes of interpretation every time we respond to the various ordinary signs around us, but in the case of our response to the Word we are called to respond with the fullness of our being. That means responding not only intellectually, with interpretative thoughts, but also emotionally and practically with interpretative feelings and interpretative actions. The eternal life of the Trinity involves the fullness of the Word and Spirit in their representation and interpretation of the being of the Father. Full participation in the divine life therefore requires the engagement of our whole selves. The more fully our interpretative responses to the Word complement and replicate the Spirit's work of interpretation, the more fully we will be incorporated into the divine life. The fullness of our interpretative response is brought forth when we strive to respond to the Word with the best of our thoughts, the deepest of our feelings, and the noblest of our actions.

⚜

We can take the next step towards seeing how we come to participate in God's life if we remember that every interpretation involves a response, a change in state of the interpreter. Whether the interpretative response is a feeling, a thought or an action, the interpreter changes in some way. The interpreter is now feeling, thinking or doing something that they were not before. When an interpreter changes state in this way the change, or the new state itself, can in turn be interpreted as a sign.

It follows that when the Spirit interprets the Word as a sign of the Father there must be some 'change' in the Spirit.[1] However, within the eternal Godhead there can be no imperfection. Therefore, if the Spirit interprets the Word, then any change in state that she undergoes in doing so cannot become a sign of anything less than the perfect goodness of the Father, as already represented by the Word. In which case, we must say that the eternal dynamic of the Spirit interpreting the Word can only ever generate further signs of the Father. The 'change' that the Spirit undergoes in interpreting the Word must result in some kind of qualitative echo of the Word. This is not to say that the Spirit simply becomes the Word, but that in interpreting the Word nothing is generated that is not further interpretable as an exact likeness of the Father.

This means, astonishingly, that if we truly adopt the place of the Spirit in interpreting the Word, we must be thereby transformed into a likeness of the Word, who is the perfect representation of the Father. This is indeed what Scripture says:

> What we do know is this: when he is revealed, we will be like him, for we will see him as he is. And all who have this hope in him purify themselves, just as he is pure. (1 John 3: 2-3)[2]

---

1 I put 'change' in inverted commas here because in the eternal life of the Trinity it is not entirely clear what change can mean. But this is not a new problem, and it is impossible to speak of God's life, or the dynamic of the mutual indwelling of the trinitarian persons, without using some kind of language of change.

2 See also Romans 8: 29; 1 Corinthians 15: 49; 2 Corinthians 3: 18.

If we become transformed into a likeness of Jesus, the Word, we are adopted into the place of the Word within the eternal Trinity. If we ourselves become like the Word, then the Spirit may interpret us truly as a sign, an image of the Father. So the process of participation in God's life begins when we take the Spirit's role, interpreting the Word as a sign of what God is like. In doing so, we are ourselves transformed into signs of what God is like, and become available as signs to be interpreted. When the Spirit interprets us as signs (even if incomplete ones) of God's quality of love, we become further incorporated into the Trinity in the place eternally occupied by the Word.

❀

What is the role of the sacraments in our adoption into God's divine life? According to one definition, a sacrament is a visible sign of an invisible grace. A fuller definition, which does not contradict the first, is that a sacrament is a sign that causes the grace that it signifies.[3] I am going to rephrase this slightly and say that a sacrament *actualizes* what it signifies. I prefer the word 'actualize' in this context because it emphasizes that we mean that a sacrament *causes to become actual* the thing that it signifies.

Two things are actualized when a sign is formed and interpreted. The first is whatever the sign is in itself. The second is whatever interpretative response is made to it. But it can immediately be seen that various kinds of sign and interpretative response might actualize what they signify, and not all are called sacraments. For example, a kiss can signify the love between two people. The love is represented by the kiss. But the kiss is also an actualization, an embodiment, of that love.

A sacrament, then, may indeed be a form of signification that follows this pattern of causing what it signifies to become actual, but it must presumably be something more (unless we want to call kisses sacraments, which perhaps in a sense they are). The something more is that a sacrament is a sign that actualizes what it signifies, *where what it signifies is the gift of participation in the divine life*. In other words, we may say that a sacrament is something (a sign) that incorporates its makers or interpreters into the life of God. And since the makers of the sacramental sign are also its (primary) interpreters, these two aspects (making and interpreting the sacramental sign) tend to converge.

---

3 The first definition is a paraphrase of something Augustine says in *On the Catechising of the Uninstructed* (26.50). The second is articulated by Thomas Aquinas in his *Summa Theologiae* (III.62.3 and Suppl. III.30.1).

Let us see how this works in the case of the sacrament of the Eucharist. The Eucharist signifies the Kingdom of God. It represents the kind of unconditional, grace-dependent fellowship that Jesus modelled and inaugurated in his ministry as a whole. But it not only represents that transformative table fellowship, it also creates that fellowship: it creates the community of the Kingdom. In that respect the Eucharist is, in a sense, no different from any meal shared by family or friends. An everyday meal is often a sign of the bonds of kinship, friendship and love. But an ordinary meal can also be a means by which such bonds are formed. Gathering around a table and eating together is a sign of friendship, trust, and forgiveness, but the sign constituted by such an act of table fellowship is also one of the ways in which these things grow and become real.

The Eucharist is no different to an everyday meal in the way that it actualizes what it signifies. The difference lies in what exactly is actualized. The function of the Eucharist beyond the significance of an ordinary meal is to shape the participants into the community of the Kingdom. That which is signified and actualized is the Kingdom of God.[4]

This difference between the Eucharist and an ordinary meal arises because the eucharistic meal is an interpretative response to the life, death and resurrection of Jesus. It is the response that Jesus asked his followers to continue to make in memory of him. In other words, the Eucharist is an interpretative response to the Word. This means that the eucharistic sign is itself an interpretative response to another sign, the Word. That is why in our liturgies the ministry of the Word precedes the ministry of the sacrament. Furthermore, our eucharistic response to the Word engages the fullness of our being: thoughts, feelings and actions. We have already seen that when we properly interpret the Word as a sign of the Father with the fullness of our being we are adopting (or being adopted into) the place of the Spirit within the Trinity. Therefore, we may say that our eucharistic response to the Word actualizes the Kingdom of God by incorporating us into God's very being. The Eucharist is a collective interpretative response to the Word that makes us "partakers of the divine nature."

We have also seen that when we fully and properly respond to the Word as the perfect representation of the Father, we are

---

4 Of course, as well as recalling Jesus' table fellowship it recalls his self-sacrifice on the Cross, to which I will turn in Chapter 8.

transformed into a likeness of the Word. It follows that the eucharistic interpretative act results in a transformation of the participants into a likeness of Christ. And since the eucharistic action is a collective action, it follows that this likeness is a collective likeness.

To reiterate why this is so: by making an interpretative response to the Word we are collectively transformed into a further sign. Any interpretative response changes the interpreter in some way, and thereby potentially makes the interpreter into a new sign of some kind or another. But when the Spirit interprets the Word as a sign of the Father there is only one new sign that can arise: an echo, a re-presentation, of the Word. In the Eucharist the participants are adopting the role of the Spirit by making an interpretative response to the Word. By making the eucharistic sign we are incorporated into the triune divine life – first by taking the place of the Spirit as interpreters of the Word, and then by being transformed as a result into a collective re-presentation of the Word, a likeness of Christ.

"Now you are the body of Christ and individually members of it," says Paul (1 Corinthians 12: 27). Just as the quality of God was embodied in the human person of Jesus, so a properly directed response to this quali-sign of the Father cannot fail to result in the transformation of the participants into a collective embodiment of that same quality. The church is called to be the embodiment of the transforming presence of God that Jesus himself embodied. "You are the light of the world. A city built on a hill cannot be hidden" (Matthew 5: 14); cf. "I am the light of the world. Whoever follows me will never walk in darkness but will have the light of life" (John 8: 12). By responding to the one Word we are incorporated into God's own life and become, collectively, an expression of that same Word.

❀

The Eucharist is the mould in which our collective embodiment as the quality of God's transforming love takes shape. Is that all there is to the actualization of the Kingdom of God?

Clearly not. The Eucharist has a particular role in actualizing the Kingdom, but it is not the sum-total of the Kingdom's actualization. So what is the Eucharist's particular role within the wider perspective of the coming Kingdom?

One of my first chemistry practicals at secondary school involved growing an alum crystal. We were instructed on how to make a saturated solution of potassium aluminium sulphate into which we dangled a short piece of string. Over a period of a few days, a perfectly formed crystal began to grow. An initially microscopic precipitation of crystalline structure at the end of the piece of string had gone on to provide the template for further growth according to the same pattern.

The formation of a crystal offers an analogy for the role of the Eucharist: the Eucharist is a template around which certain forms of relationship can be shaped in such a way as to actualize the Kingdom of God. A difference is that crystal growth simply involves adding more of the same, whereas the growth of the Kingdom may take many different forms. The Eucharist can seed and shape the growth of those forms of participation in the divine life, just as the initial crystallization around the string seeds and shapes the subsequent growth of the crystal.

A key concept to consider here is the formation of habits. We tend to regard habits as blind propensities to repeat certain behaviours. Going to church merely out of habit may sound like a bad thing, which indeed it may be. But habits can also be the ultimate form of interpretation. We have seen that interpretations can be feelings or actions as well as thoughts. It is not surprising, then, that we can develop habits of thought, habits of feeling and habits of action. Such interpretative habits can be honed and refined by monitoring their adequacy as ways of making sense of the world. They are tried and tested patterns of behaviour that help us to navigate the sea of signs.

The fact that interpretative responses can be habitual doesn't mean they are dead or mindless. Habits can be living and dynamic. Complex dynamic systems in the physical world show an analogous kind of habit-formation. Think of the patterns of currents and eddies in a fast-flowing stream. The movement of the water is entrained into certain kinds of recurring pattern by meeting the shapes and obstructions of the river bed. In physics the relatively stable patterns that arise in complex systems are called 'attractors'. Attractors are not immutable. If the shape of the river bed changes or the flow of water increases or decreases, different kinds of flow patterns will arise. Likewise, some habits of interpretation that have been stable and effective for a long time may need to be revised and reshaped in response to changing circumstances. A certain kind of interpretative habit may cease to be appropriate in the light, for example, of a new scientific discovery or a fresh moral insight.

The important point here is that interpretative habits can be tested for their continuing capacity to help us make our way in the world.

Habits must be responsive to the way that the world really is. If they don't conform to the bedrock of reality, they won't ultimately turn out to be stable. The pace of change may be slower than the changes of habit of water-flow in a stream, but interpretative habits can nevertheless evolve to track reality.

Habits, then, are very ordinary, practical propensities of behaviour, but they are also important modes of interpretation. It is no accident that C.S. Peirce, the founder of the school of semiotic theory on which this book draws, was also the founder of the philosophical school of 'pragmatism'. Pragmatism holds that the meaning of a concept is ultimately given by the sum of its practical effects. The practical consequences of concepts are reflected in the habits of interpretation to which they give rise. When interpretations regularly match the way things actually are, they become habitual. According to Peirce, the 'ultimate interpretants' of signs – the kinds of interpretation that can bring a sequence of interpretations to an end – are habits. So the ultimate forms of interpretation are not mystical flights of fancy or highly abstract forms of conceptualization. Interpretation terminates in ordinary, concrete, embodied habits of action.

Part of the purpose of the Eucharist, I believe, is to entrain certain kinds of 'ultimate' interpretative habit. The Eucharist is the seed, the initial disturbance of symmetry (to echo the language of chaos theory's account of the origins of pattern formation) around which the interpretative habits of Christian discipleship begin to form. John's Gospel surely reflects this when the story of the institution of the Eucharist at the Last Supper is replaced by the account of Jesus washing the disciples' feet. After doing so, Jesus says to them:

> So if I, your Lord and Teacher, have washed your feet, you also ought to wash one another's feet. For I have set you an example, that you also should do as I have done to you. (John 13: 14-15)

To summarize, we become partakers of the divine nature by responding to the Word with the fullness of our being, and thereby being adopted into the place of the Spirit. In making such interpretative responses to the Word we are transformed, by virtue of the logic of the divine perfection, into the image of the one to whom we are responding. The interpretative habits that are entrained by participation in the sacraments, especially the sacrament of the Eucharist, are what give some degree of stability and continuity (though not absolute imperviousness to change) to the church which is thereby constituted as the body of Christ.

7

Holding the Baby

As we have seen in Chapter 6, when we interpret the Word as a sign of God the Father we are, as creatures, doing what the Spirit does within the eternal Trinity. By grace we are thus adopted into the place of the Spirit within the divine life.

To recap, with any interpretation, our interpretative response to the Word changes us in some way: it transforms us. Anything can be a sign in one way or another, so any change that we undergo means that we can ourselves become a new or changed sign of something. We have seen, that within the eternal Trinity, if the Spirit becomes a new sign this cannot be a sign that is in any way less than a perfect likeness of the Father, which is what the Word already is. Anything less would mean that the eternal Trinity would become degraded by living its own life. It follows that if we creatures adopt, or are adopted into, the place of the Spirit then any consequent change in us in the form of an interpretative response to the Word must result in a transformation of ourselves towards better or fuller likenesses of the Word. As we have seen, that is why when we respond to the Word in the eucharistic act we collectively become the body of Christ.

The transformation of the interpreting entity into a likeness of the sign that it interprets is, of course, not what usually happens in an interpretation. It is peculiar to the act of partaking in the divine nature; a peculiarity that arises from God's non-degradable goodness. There are many kinds of creaturely interpretative response that do not conform to this pattern, including any kind of response that does not have effects consonant with God's ultimate loving purposes. However, any proper response to the Word as a perfect sign of the Father must follow this pattern: adoption into the place of the Spirit and transformation into a likeness of the Word.

In this chapter, I want to add a third principle. At first sight it is rather simple, but its addition will have important repercussions. The additional principle is that something of the dynamic of God's eternal self-interpretation can be activated whenever we recognize anything in the world as, in some respect, a sign or image of God.

Think, for example, of the life of a saint. Such a life may image God in a way that is recognizably similar to the way in which Jesus images the Father. On the other hand, something much simpler than a human life may also image God in some respect. Suppose, for example, that I find myself contemplating the beauty of a bluebell. The perfection of the flower may call to mind the perfection of the divine nature. Even more simply, the quality of the blueness of the bluebell may remind me that, just as the bluebell embodies certain qualities, so God has a unique quality of God's own: the quality of love. Indeed, God must be the ground of the possibility of any quality whatsoever, otherwise God would not be the sovereign Creator of everything. In noticing the quality of the blue of the bluebell I am responding not only to a particular quality, but also to a sign that qualities are possible at all. And in doing so I have an opportunity to acknowledge the ultimate ground of all qualities.

When we interpret something in the world as partially or indirectly imaging God we are again adopting the place of the Spirit within the Trinity. It is the role of the Spirit to be the eternally active interpreter of that which images God the Father (which, within the eternal Trinity, is the Word). We must therefore say that, just as interpreting the perfect Word of the Father draws us into the life of God, so responding to anything else that at least partially images the Father can likewise make us partakers of the divine nature. In effect, we are seeing the world as the Spirit sees the world, and this puts us into the place of the Spirit.

It seems to me, further, that when we recognize a partial likeness to God (the Father) in something or someone, we are drawing that thing (or person) into the divine life. Something that is able to reveal an aspect of the Father's quality to us stands in a place equivalent to that of the Word within the Trinity. We take on the role of the Spirit, recognizing something as in some way imaging the Father, and we are therefore adopting that thing or person into the place occupied within the eternal Trinity by the Word. In other words, we can participate in the divine life not only by recognizing and responding to the Word as presented to us in Scripture but also by responding to things in the world that in some way image God.

There are, then, three ways in which our interpretative responses can make us partakers of the divine nature. First, when we interpret the Word as the image of the Father, we are being adopted into the place of the Spirit. Second, when we make such an interpretative response we are changed, at least in some small way, and such a change must – because of the perfection of the eternal divine act of representation and interpretation – cause us to be formed into a closer likeness of the Word. Third, when we rightly interpret anything in the world as even a partial or indirect image of God's nature we are drawn into the life of God because we are seeing things as the Spirit does. Furthermore, the thing or person that we are interpreting as an image of the Father is thereby also drawn into the divine life because we are, in doing so, adopting it or them into the place of the Word.

But now things get complicated, for the world is not static, but always changing. The signs that the world presents to us are forever on the move. Moreover, we are creatures who are not only good at recognizing signs, but also skilled at making them; so it is within our power to make new images of God in the world. And that means that we are capable of giving ourselves – and the world – a leg up into the divine life!

Two examples of ways in which we pursue such sign-making in a more or less formalized way are gardening and art. It is often remarked that gardens feature prominently in the Bible. Genesis starts in one and the Gospels reach their climax in another. In our gardens we attempt to shape the stuff of the world into something beautiful. And whether we're creating a geometrically perfect formal garden, or a chaotic wildflower.meadow, we are making something that has the potential – whether or not this is our conscious intention – to image the nature of God.

If contemplation of the blueness of the bluebell offers me a route into participation in God's life, then so does contemplation of my garden as a whole. The difference is that I did not make the shape or colour of the bluebell, but I did (in some sense) create the shape and colour of my garden. We should therefore not shy away from saying that our (God-given) capacity for making things offers a foot-hold on the path to participation in the divine life. We can, as it were, 'lever' our way into the eternal dynamic of the Trinity. The fulcrum of this leverage can be something we have come across (like a bluebell) or something we have ourselves made (like a flower bed). All that is required is that the point around which this movement turns in some way takes the place of the Word by (somehow and partially) imaging the Father. Our own creative capabilities enable us to be active, rather than merely passive, participants in this process.

Gardening, of course, requires both the work of the gardener and the grace of God – the latter in allowing the plants to grow and flourish. Art, in apparent contrast, usually involves working *inanimate* stuff into signs. The kinds of sign may be explicitly representational or highly abstract. And of course art does not always attempt to represent God. But by creating novel images or objects it always, at least indirectly, has the potential to image something of the quality of God, just as the bluebell does.[1]

Art, more than gardening, has at times been regarded with great suspicion by theologians and religious authorities. The iconoclasts' contention is that any attempt to make an image of God is inherently sinful and doomed to failure: doomed because it is not within our capabilities to make an image of the eternal and utterly transcendent Creator of everything, and sinful because it is dangerous to think otherwise. There is undeniably a grain of truth in this. Mistakenly taking something for an image of God is idolatry, arguably the root of all sinfulness. And thinking that we can acquire knowledge of God by our own efforts, independent of God's grace, is rightly regarded as heresy.

I have chosen to speak in terms of giving ourselves a 'leg up' into the divine life, of gaining some 'leverage' on the dynamic of the Trinity. In doing so I am well aware that I will risk offending certain theological sensibilities; indeed, I am probably being deliberately provocative. Nevertheless, I regard it as appropriate to speak in such terms because I do so in the context of a strong affirmation that things are so only because God has graciously willed them to be so. Human creativity has a capacity positively to contribute to the dynamic of our own participation in the divine life only because of God's unconditional gift of such a capacity. Misrepresenting God is sinful, I think, not because attempting to represent God is inherently sinful, but because truly representing God takes us so close to the heart of God's purposes for the world. Representation and misrepresentation of God matter so much because God's very being is inherently representational.

We must also remember that when we interpret things in the world as images of God, the Word itself is not a passive bystander. The meaning of a sign can be altered by its context. For Christians, the context of all our responses to the world is the life, death and

---

1 It is worth noting that when we respond to works of art – whether visual, literary or musical – we may have a sense of being absorbed into the immediate presence of the object or quality in question. There is a sense, then, in which art and our responses to it involve some kind of 'collapse' of the sign, object and interpretative response into one another. I suspect this may offer a hint about what ultimately it is like to be drawn into God's presence through our responses to signs, though I do not wish to imply that our own individual realities will be lost by dissolving into God.

resurrection of Jesus. The Word illuminates the world and casts it in a new light. It is not surprising that the prologue to John's Gospel refers to Christ as the Word and also, in the same breath, calls him the light (John 1: 4-5). In this light, things not previously recognized as images of God will now be recognized:

> Then the righteous will answer him, "Lord, when was it that we saw you hungry and gave you food, or thirsty and gave you something to drink?" . . . And the king will answer them, "Truly I tell you, just as you did it to one of the least of these who are members of my family, you did it to me." (Matthew 25: 37-40)

The light not only illuminates existing signs, it helps us to form new ones. I have mentioned gardening and art as examples, but the relation of our sign-making to the Kingdom of God is not limited to these. Ideas and intentions are signs. When we imagine a different world we *image* it in our minds. Making and recognizing likenesses of God in the world is a way of actualizing our incorporation into the life and Kingdom of God, and so is imaging God and God's purposes in our minds. An abstract idea, such as justice or liberty, can be as effective a force in the world as the most physical of causes. When we form and respond to such concepts, with consequences great or small, we are doing something equivalent to making and responding to the beauty of a garden or a work of art. We are becoming incorporated into the life of God by creating mental signs that occupy the place of the Word, and interpreting them through the power of the Spirit.

Of course, the mode of interpretative response involved may be different in each of these examples. If I contemplate my garden, I may be filled with a warm feeling – an emotional form of interpretation (and no less an indication of being drawn into the divine nature for being so). If, on the other hand, I form a conception of justice in my mind and respond to it with an interpretative action, I may find myself manning the barricades or serving at a soup kitchen. As we have seen, our fullest participation in God's life occurs when we employ the whole range of our modes of interpretative response – feelings, actions and thoughts.

In all of this I am not saying anything new about gardening or art, justice or liberty. What I am inviting you to do is to see that we have a God-given capacity to become partakers in the divine nature. There is a simple pattern behind all the diverse ways in which this can occur. The pattern depends upon three factors: 1. When we interpret the Word as a sign of the Father, we are adopted into the place held by the Spirit within the eternal Trinity. 2. When, by taking the place of the Spirit, we interpret the Word as an image of the Father we are ourselves transformed into closer likenesses of the Word. 3. This process of '*theosis* by semiosis' (becoming incorporated into the divine nature through the processes of signification and interpretation) can start when we respond to (interpret) the ordinary things of the world.

❁

To complete our understanding of the way in which our capacity for representation and interpretation is the basis of our participation in the divine nature, we must take note of one further level of complexity: we can interpret the gardens or works of art that we create, but they do not interpret us.[2] However, we can nurture one another to become closer likenesses of the divine nature, and when we recognize another person as an image of God, that person is able to reciprocate.

When we take the place of the Spirit in interpreting the Word we are transformed into a closer likeness of the Word, and it follows that this reciprocal kind of imaging and interpreting that can occur between people can become a runaway process. When two lovers gaze into each other's faces, the delight on the one's face is interpreted by the other as a sign of their own worth, which in turn causes their own face to light up, and so on. In science, these kinds of processes are called positive feedback loops. Something like this happens as we help one another into the Kingdom. This is hinted at in the following striking, but somewhat puzzling, passage from Paul's Second Letter to the Corinthians:

> And all of us, with unveiled faces, seeing the glory of the Lord as though reflected in a mirror, are being transformed into the same image from one degree of glory to another; for this comes from the Lord, the Spirit. (2 Corinthians 3: 18)

I say that this is puzzling because it isn't immediately obvious who is supposed to be reflected in the mirror. If we look in a mirror we see ourselves, not someone else. It is not clear why looking in a mirror would help us see Christ, let alone be transformed into his likeness.

---

2 We may find ourselves reinterpreting ourselves or being reinterpreted by others in their light, but that is not the same as saying that the garden or the art is itself an actively interpretative entity.

The reference to 'unveiled faces' alludes to the veil that Moses put over his face to protect the Israelites from seeing the full glory of God, recalled in the verses preceding these. There is naturally a tendency to read the passage, therefore, as being about seeing clearly the glory of God. But I suggest that there is more to it than this. The passage is about the runaway process of imaging and interpretation that enables us to become partakers of the divine nature. Paul suggests that the veil lies not only over Moses' *face*, but also over the *minds* of those reading the 'old covenant' (2 Corinthians 3: 15). In other words, the veil lies over the interpretation as well as the image. The veil is anything that dulls and dampens the reciprocal processes of image-making and image-interpretation. If the process is dampened it cannot take on the self-reinforcing, runaway character that enables it to be our 'leg up' into the divine life. When the veil was over Moses' face the glory was being "set aside" (2 Corinthians 3: 7, New Revised Standard Version) it was "soon to fade" (Revised English Bible). When the veil is removed we are able to be transformed "from one degree of glory to another."

The point here is therefore not just, or primarily, about clarity of vision. It is about the dynamics of the processes of representation and interpretation. Reflections in a mirror are an analogy for this to-and-fro dynamic (think of our lovers gazing into each other's eyes). And these processes do not have to start from gazing on the face of Jesus himself (cf. 2 Corinthians 4: 6), but can do so from anything that even partially images his 'face'. For, as we have seen above, when we rightly interpret things in the world as partial images of God we adopt the interpretative place of the Spirit, and in doing so are transformed little by little into a likeness of the Word.

We are all "being transformed into the same image from one degree of glory to another." However, these reciprocal processes would be mere wheels within wheels, empty mechanisms, if it were not for the fact that, as Paul makes sure to remind us a few verses later, the good news is that the glory of Christ, the image into whose likeness we are being transformed, is precisely "the image of God" (2 Corinthians 4: 4; cf. Colossians 1: 15). The fact that the Word is the perfect image of the invisible God guarantees that in being transformed from one degree of glory to another we are not merely going round in interpretative circles, but are being enabled to become partakers of the divine nature.

❋

Our daughter was born while I was a medical student. I had just started my obstetric attachment and my wife was very keen for me to be present at our own child's birth before I was involved in delivering any other babies. By a matter of days, that is how it worked out. I remember at some point in her first few days of life holding our baby daughter and telling her that she was very precious and that I would never do anything that would harm her. Having that little new life in my hands was changing me – changing my perspectives and priorities, my aims and my hopes.

Anyone who has been present at a birth may well have had a similar experience. Even if you have not been present when a baby has been born you may be aware of having been affected in some way by the arrival of a new person in your family or social circle. I want to suggest that such experiences are relevant to thinking about the sacrament of baptism. I suggest, further, that the runaway dynamic of representation and interpretation that we have been considering is important to understanding what baptism is about.

The obvious reference of the sign of baptism is to new birth. The candidate is immersed in water, just as the baby is immersed in amniotic fluid. He or she then emerges, born afresh into the world to begin a new kind of life. Baptism and Eucharist are the two 'dominical' sacraments – the two sacraments of the church with a claim to having been instituted by Jesus. But I think the usual accounts of baptism as a sacrament are puzzling. It was stated earlier that a sacrament is a sign that actualizes what it signifies. Further, a sacrament brings into actuality the Kingdom of God. This is what distinguishes sacraments from other kinds of sign, such as kisses, which may also actualize what they signify. In the case of the Eucharist, the meal signifies, let us say, the heavenly banquet. But it also actualizes the heavenly banquet in the sense that the kind of loving, forgiving, fellowship involved in the formation of the eucharistic sign is precisely an actualization of the Kingdom.

The problem with the usual accounts of baptism is that they do not clearly explain how baptism actualizes what it signifies, if what is actualized must be the Kingdom of God. Of course, you can give an account that seems to achieve this. What is signified is new birth, and what is actualized is the candidate's entry into their new family, the family of the church. But in what sense is this entry into membership of the community of faith *actualized* by the enactment of this rebirth? Perhaps entry into the community is understood as being actualized in the sense that this is the rite of passage that is necessary to obtain membership. But this does not seem to give us the same kind of intrinsic relation between the sign and the thing actualized as in the case of the Eucharist. In the Eucharist an ordinary familiar event, a meal which, in its everyday form, is capable of actualizing and maintaining certain kinds of relationship between the participants, becomes a way of actualizing the forms of relationship that constitute the Kingdom of God. But the same is not true of baptism, at least by most accounts. In other words, it is not clear in what sense baptism actually *causes* a new situation to come into effect, beyond being a *marker* of entry into membership of the church. Why wouldn't some other ritual, preferably with an element of scriptural allusion, be just as suitable? To answer that baptizing people is what Jesus instructed us to do does not solve the problem, because without an account of how the sacrament of baptism actualizes what it signifies – namely, the Kingdom of God – Jesus' instruction would appear arbitrary. Baptism would then be a sign of entry into the family of the church only in the superficial sense that it offers the badge of membership, rather than any deep sense that the sacrament *causes* that membership to become real.

I rather suspect that liturgists have been at least subconsciously aware of this deficiency in standard accounts of baptism. The Church of England's Common Worship baptism service, for example, is notoriously wordy. In my experience, the sacrament very often seems like a rather disconnected sequence of little rituals – lighting a candle, signing with the cross, wetting with water, anointing with oil – each one needing its own little explanation, all in the desperate hope that the whole will add up to more than the sum of the parts.

All of this makes me wonder whether we are missing something. Perhaps we are inclined to see the importance of baptism too much from the point of view of the candidate (though I do not for a moment wish to diminish its significance for the individual believer). This is where I think the experience of witnessing a birth, or at least of being changed by the arrival of a new life in the world, may be instructive. Baptism would make sense as a sign that actualizes what it signifies if what it actualizes is not primarily something in the candidate, but something in the witnesses. Just as the witnesses to an ordinary birth (or those closely affected by the birth) may be transformed by the event, so the church is transformed by witnessing the birth of a new member into its midst. We, the witnesses, are obliged to consider what kind of care and nurturing of fellow members of our community is appropriate to the actualization of God's purposes. In enacting such care and nurturing (both individually and in the overall structure and dynamic of the community) we will be actualizing the Kingdom of God.

At the sacrament of baptism, the church ought to review, renew and if necessary reform its habits of fellowship and discipleship. This renewal and reformation is an interpretative response to the sign of new birth, just as was my response to holding my new-born daughter. The transformation that is brought about in the witnesses to a baptism is essentially the same kind of transformation that may occur in response to an ordinary birth. But this transformation is, beyond this, an actualization of the Kingdom because (like the Eucharist) baptism is itself an interpretative response to the Word. Specifically, it is an interpretative response to the Word's call to us to be formed into a new kind of family in a new kind of world. During baptism (whether of a child or an adult) we re-enact a birth in such a way that the family that is thereby constituted, or reconstituted, is the family of the church, the community that is committed to actualizing the Kingdom which was proclaimed and inaugurated by the incarnate Word.

In this, the parents and godparents are, of course, representatives of the whole body of the church: it is the whole church that must rethink its purposes and priorities whenever it welcomes a new member. As at an ordinary birth the event is of immeasurable significance to the person being born. But that is the sum of what is happening to them – they are simply being born, marvellous though that is. The church, on the other hand, is being *transformed* by witnessing the birth. That, I think, is what makes baptism a sacrament: a sign that signifies and actualizes the commitment of the church to form an environment in which others may receive the grace of God. If it is objected that this is not the church's traditional understanding of baptism, I reply that it must have been implicitly so for as long as we have been baptizing infants. For, whatever other justifications for infant baptism may be produced, a key consequence of baptizing young children is to make baptism a (relatively) passive act from the candidate's point of view and an active transformative act for the witnesses.

On the view that I have offered here, it may be seen that baptism is complementary to the Eucharist. The Eucharist is the everyday sacrament that keeps the church functioning, just as regularly sitting down at a table for a meal can help keep a family functioning. Baptism is the occasional sacrament that should signify *and actualize* the renewal of the church, just as an ordinary birth can prompt a change in the dynamics of a family or a rethink of its purposes and priorities. But this complementarity is not simply a matter of the two sacraments fulfilling a pair of jointly necessary functions. Rather, the function of each is intertwined with the other. The analogy drawn with birth and family mealtimes remains pertinent here. Our children are always welcome at the family table precisely because they are the ones who transformed our lives by being born into the family. And, conversely, we allowed these children to turn our lives upside down when they were born precisely because we knew that these were the ones who would always have a place at our table.

It may now be evident that my reflections earlier in this chapter on the active, dynamic, reciprocal process of divine image-making and image-interpretation were preparatory to this view of the sacrament of baptism. The process acknowledged, stimulated and actualized by bearing witness to a baptism is the process of continually working out our understanding of what it is to image God and to respond to images of God. The community of the church should be perpetually challenged, renewed and redirected by engaging in this process. It is the sacrament of baptism that should concretely entrain this process within the life of the church.

If the only sacrament we had was the Eucharist, the church would be in danger of thinking that all that is needed for the actualization of the Kingdom of God is faithful adherence to existing practices and understandings. Baptism ensures that the dynamic of the church is one of active learning and growth, not passive repetition. The point of baptism is nothing less than fuelling the runaway process that can be described as "seeing the glory of the Lord as though reflected in a mirror," so as to ensure that "all of us . . . are being transformed into the same image from one degree of glory to another."

8

The Joy of Scapegoating

Once when I telephoned my brother and his wife in New York they described to me the scene in their small Manhattan apartment. Their children had just received delivery of a large box of second-hand Lego and the floor was covered with the assorted pieces. Parents and children were now sifting through the mess trying to work out how much of the Lego, if any, belonged to particular special sets (the farmyard set, the police helicopter set?). Without any of the original packaging, it was difficult to know whether any of the jumble of pieces on the floor could be tied together by an overall theme and how much was simply generic Lego, ready to be built into whatever they wanted.

The church has faced a similar dilemma when confronted by theories of atonement. Over the centuries Christians have accumulated quite a jumble of ideas about how Jesus' life, death and resurrection can effect our salvation – our reconciliation (at-one-ment) with God. Some Christians understand the Cross as a punishment deserved by all humanity, which Jesus, though himself entirely innocent, has received in our place. Sometimes, on the other hand, the Cross has been understood as a price paid as a ransom to the devil. Alternatively, Jesus' crucifixion can be seen as a victory in the battle between good and evil. It may also be regarded as a definitive example and demonstration of how humans ought to live in loving service to one another.

Some basis for each of these theories can be found in Scripture. It is notable, however, that the church's official doctrines have never given ultimate approval to any of these theories over the others. Atonement theories in classical church teaching are like a collection of generic Lego, ready to be put together in whatever way we can, but not conforming to any overarching structure or pre-existing framework.

One particular version of atonement theory tends to polarize opinion in the church. This is the penal substitution theory: the idea that the innocent Jesus took upon himself a punishment that ought to have been suffered by the rest of us sinners. In some strands of theological tradition this theory is understood as the key to atonement, and indeed the key to the Christian faith. Others, myself included, regard this as a relatively late and somewhat unsavoury development in Christian thinking. For what sort of god would really be so obsessed with punishing sin that they would be willing to inflict horrendous pain on their innocent Son? Such a god would appear to be cruel and vindictive; even, as has often been pointed out, a child abuser. But if the Cross cannot reasonably be understood in this way, the question arises: How central is the Cross to atonement? Might it be that the Incarnation, rather than the crucifixion, was the really necessary thing? Couldn't Jesus' participation in humanity's sufferings have been just as much the basis of salvation, perhaps more so, if he had died of old age or dementia?

Until fairly recently my own views on atonement theory leant towards the 'generic Lego' rather than the 'specific package' approach. I have since changed my mind on this, largely as a result of coming across a relatively new way of thinking about atonement (though it is one that is arguably implicit in the entire witness of the Judaeo-Christian Scriptures). As a consequence, I have come to think that there is, after all, one overarching theory of atonement that can hold the various other models together. Furthermore, it turns out that the Cross is, after all, crucial.

This new way of thinking about atonement draws particularly on the ideas of the contemporary French-born philosopher, René Girard.[1] Central to Girard's thought is the idea of scapegoating, and for convenience I will refer to the whole approach as the scapegoating theory of atonement. The scapegoating theory has two main parts. The first part is the claim that scapegoating is a fundamental part of the structure of human societies. In other words, Girard suggests that our tendency to blame individuals or groups for things for which they are not really responsible is not merely a regrettable human weakness; it performs a powerful function in stabilizing human groups and communities. The second part of the scapegoating theory of atonement is that Jesus' life, including his death on the Cross, offers a way out of these structures of blame and victimization and hence offers the possibility of being reconciled with God.

The scapegoating conceptualization emphasizes the importance of imitation, or mimesis, in the formation of human patterns of behaviour. The idea is that we are biologically predisposed to

---

1 See, for example, René Girard, *I See Satan Fall Like Lightning* (Maryknoll, New York: Orbis Books and Leominster: Gracewing, translated by James G. Williams, 2001); James Alison, *Raising Abel: The Recovery of the Eschatological Imagination* (London: SPCK, second edition 2010, first published 1996).

imitate those around us. Anyone who has watched a very small baby imitating the facial expressions of their parent – smiling, laughing, sticking their tongue out – can hardly doubt that there is something in this. Mimesis makes good biological sense: an efficient way of learning important and complex survival strategies is to take the behaviour of other members of our species as a model. Indeed, as I remarked in Chapter 5, some very interesting evidence is emerging about the brain mechanisms that underlie these remarkable capabilities. By imitation we often come to desire the same things as those around us, even when those things do not ultimately lead to human fulfilment. Our competitive desires cause tensions to build up within groups and societies, which then require some mechanism for their dissipation.

According to scapegoating theory, one of the things we are very good at learning is how to pick out individual people or groups of people to victimize. This isn't very nice for the victims, but it is 'good' for society as a whole. Why? Because it provides just such a mechanism: it relieves the accumulated tension between members of the group, releasing dangerous energy in the form of the apparently acceptable violence of exclusion, establishing a common cause against whichever individual or group has been chosen to be excluded or victimized.

One of the reasons that I find the scapegoating theory so compelling is that it is easy to see this mechanism at work in our own lives. Something as simple as laughing with a group of friends at someone else's expense – a little bit of bonding achieved by some minor criticism of someone's habits – is an example of the scapegoating mechanism in action. On a larger scale, in our workplaces, is it not tempting to find someone to blame for problems that really have a more systemic origin? In our families, how often does blame for everyone's dysfunction get heaped on one family member? And in society? Within the church? I'll leave you to make your own confession; I plead shamefully guilty.

Two aspects of the scapegoating theory must be emphasized. First, a scapegoat does not necessarily have to be entirely innocent. The mechanism works by blaming people for things for which they are not entirely responsible. They may be legitimately to blame for other things, or for part of that with which they are accused; but the mechanism works by blaming them for more than they deserve, for sending them off to carry responsibility for things for which responsibility really lies (at least partly) within the victimizing group.

Second, the victimizers are not usually explicitly aware of what they are doing. Indeed, the mechanism only really works if it is invisible to those involved in it. The victimizers are convinced that what they are doing is right and just, and they feel good about it. It's the feeling good about it that makes us behave like this. Just as the pleasure of sex has evolved because it helps to perpetuate the species, so the 'joy' of scapegoating is our immediate motivation for acting as victimizers. We experience the pleasure of blaming (the 'proximate' mechanism) without being aware that the real ('ultimate') reason for the existence of the scapegoating mechanism is that it stabilizes society. Hence, perhaps, Jesus' otherwise surprising acknowledgement that the present order of things will be destabilized by his anti-scapegoating programme: "Do not think that I have come to bring peace to the earth; I have not come to bring peace, but a sword" (Matthew 10: 34).

One of the most interesting suggestions of the scapegoating theory is that the Hebrew and Christian Scriptures as a whole can be read as the story of the gradual realization (or revelation) of the truth about the innocence of victims. This is closely tied to the history of the use of sacrifices, for of course at least some forms of sacrifice involve literally the death of a chosen victim to achieve a kind of cleansing, peacemaking or reconciliation. Indeed, the word 'scapegoat' refers to the Jewish ritual on the Day of Atonement when a goat was chosen to bear the sins of the people, figuratively carrying those sins on its head as it was banished to the wilderness outside the city walls.

Most readers of this book will live in societies deeply influenced by the Judaeo-Christian tradition. Although contemporary culture often wishes to dispense with the trappings of Christianity, we usually take it to be perfectly natural and obvious that the oppressed and vulnerable should be protected. It is therefore very difficult for most of us now to understand a mindset in which those who suffer are automatically believed to be experiencing a deserved punishment. But that was exactly the default assumption of most ancient cultures. The Judaeo-Christian trajectory has predisposed us to see that God is on the side of victims and (eventually) to call into question our deeply entrenched reliance on the scapegoating mechanism. Human nature being what it is, however, we always have the capacity to subvert this revelation into other forms of evil. One such perversion is deliberately to play the role of the victim or the marginalized. Legitimate campaigning can easily turn into a further round of reverse scapegoating in which the oppressors become the ones to be blamed and excluded. The result can be an endless cycle of tit-for-tat, of blame, exclusion and violence.

According to scapegoating theory, then, the significance of the Cross is that it was the ultimate revelation and undoing of the scapegoating mechanism. It was the ultimate *revelation* of the mechanism because Jesus was demonstrably the totally innocent victim. He went to his death refusing to meet violence with violence, taking all the undeserved blame that was heaped upon him, choosing not to make further victims of his oppressors. Only when the scapegoating mechanism could be so clearly revealed as unjust was it possible for its actual function to be disclosed and recognized.

The Cross was the ultimate *undoing* of the scapegoating mechanism because the mechanism depends on being invisible. In order for it to work the participants in the scapegoating must all believe that the scapegoat deserves what they are getting. Once the innocence of the victim is out in the open, plain for all to see, the mechanism loses its power. In this light, the Cross worked not because it was the best ever sacrifice, but because, as the clearest revelation of what sacrifice is really all about, it invited and offered an end to all sacrifice.

♊

The above is the very briefest of outlines of scapegoating theory. All sorts of objections and difficulties may occur to you, in which case I would recommend turning to the various excellent books on the subject.[2] My purpose here is not to argue the full case for the theory, but to say why I think it fits especially well with the semiotic perspective we have been investigating. I must also make clear at this point that while I think the scapegoating conceptualization of atonement is consistent with the semiotic model of the Trinity, the semiotic model as a whole does not depend on the viability of the scapegoating approach. If you do not find the scapegoating theory convincing you are free to ask yourself how your own preferred approach to atonement would fit with the semiotic model. If I may dare to presume that you accept there may be something in my quali-sign account of the Incarnation, what would you want to say about the 'quality' of God that has thus been revealed in the person of Jesus? What is it about that quality that is of saving significance for humans? And what is it about that salvation that has cosmic, rather than just earthly, implications?

Let us ask these questions, then, of the scapegoating approach. To begin with, it seems to me that the scapegoating theory of

2 For example, S. Mark Heim, *Saved from Sacrifice: A Theology of the Cross* (Grand Rapids, Michigan: Eerdmans, 2006); Wolfgang Palaver, *René Girard's Mimetic Theory* (East Lansing, Michigan: Michigan State University Press, 2013).

atonement fits well with the account of Jesus' understanding of his own ministry which we touched on in Chapter 4. Jesus came to inaugurate the Kingdom of God by enacting and embodying the very presence of YHWH. We noted there that the enactment of that presence included opposition to violence as a response to the Roman occupation and table fellowship with those whom society had chosen to exclude. Forgiveness and healing came to people through Jesus' demonstration that God's Kingdom is not built and stabilized by the victimization of those who seem worthy of blame. Neither is it furthered by entering into endless cycles of retaliation and violence. The good news is that the new humanity, the new creation, no longer needs to rely on this highly effective but unjust mechanism. The mechanism is decisively revealed and undone by Jesus' own submission to it on the Cross.

If the scapegoating account of atonement fits with the idea that Jesus enacted and embodied the victorious return of YHWH (albeit that the manner of the victory was not quite as expected), then it also fits with the quali-sign understanding of the Incarnation. The quality of God that is revealed in the person of Jesus is the quality of love: the quality of the costly bearing of anything and everything for the sake of the avoidance of creating victims. It is the actual embodiment of this quality in the person of Jesus – who, though perfectly innocent, allows himself to be horrifically scapegoated – that reveals and disarms the scapegoating mechanism.

Importantly, the embodiment and revelation of this quality is both an *example* of how God's love should be enacted and the *objective realization and inauguration* of God's Kingdom. Some Christians criticize what they take to be a weak 'liberal' view that the Cross was nothing more than an exemplar – a model for how humans ought to act rather than an event that objectively changed the world. But on the scapegoating/quali-sign view, this is seen to rest on a false dichotomy. The Cross was objectively effective precisely because, in Jesus, the full quality of God's being is embodied and revealed.

An objection to my semiotic reading of the scapegoating theory of atonement (and to the quali-sign account of the Incarnation in general) could be that it is insufficiently interventionist. Traditional accounts of the Incarnation usually describe God having acted in a special way in order to become enfleshed within the world. This kind of action is usually conceived of as some sort of outside intervention that intruded into the natural order of things. According to this view, Jesus would not have been divine if God had not in some way interrupted the natural flow of events. Without such an intervention (however we understand it to have occurred), Mary's son would have been just another ordinary human being. In short, the objection that may be raised to the account of Incarnation and atonement that I have been developing in these chapters is that it leaves no room for recognizing them as instances of special divine action.

Let me offer two possible responses to this concern. Recall, if you will, the analogy I suggested in Chapter 4. There I suggested that the embodiment of the very quality of God's being within the fabric of the world might be analogous to the emergence of a particular quality during the growth of a tree: specifically, I used the example of the colour of ebony wood. The point of the analogy was that this colour is not imparted from outside, like a piece of cloth taking up a dye. Rather, the ebony colour is an intrinsic property of the wood, a quality that depends on the particular underlying structure of the material. In terms of the question of special divine action, the analogy of ebony illustrates that it may be coherent to hold the view that no such discrete intervention was needed to effect the incarnation of God's being within the natural order. Rather, the created order is understood to have a natural (but God-given) capacity to become formed into precisely the configuration – the configuration that we rightly call Incarnation – that traditional accounts say would require some kind of special outside intervention.

The first possible solution for those who wish to press the 'interventionist' objection would be simply to revert to our other analogy: that the world has precisely the properties necessary to be able to take up the quality of God's being, just as a certain kind of fabric may be needed to take up a special kind of dye. On that version the Incarnation would indeed require a direct divine intervention, an intervention that imparted the 'colour' of God's love to the fabric of the world.

If considering the latter analogy is what is required in order to keep the intervention-minded reader on board for the moment, so be it. I would prefer, however, to persuade you that there is a better way of thinking about the question of God's acts of Incarnation and atonement. So much depends on exactly what one invests in the slippery term 'natural'. Those who want the Incarnation to have involved a special instance of divine action within the natural order are, I suspect, regarding 'natural' as meaning that which to some extent normally runs along *without* any divine action. But is this the best way of understanding the ordinary running of the world? Shouldn't we, rather, suppose that every instant of existence requires God's continuous, sustaining activity? In that case, everything that occurs 'naturally' is nevertheless dependent on God's direct creative involvement. In Chapter 10 I shall suggest how this creative activity may be understood as the work of all three trinitarian persons. For the moment, let us just note that the Greek gods were continual, if capricious, interveners in the world's affairs. Only the Judaeo-Christian God has the distinction of not needing to resort to such shenanigans. As Creator of all that is, the God and Father of our Lord Jesus Christ creates and sustains the universe in a manner that lies well beyond our everyday conceptions of making or intervening.

Crucially, there is an infinite and unbridgeable conceptual difference between a world that has been granted the capacity fully and perfectly to contain an embodiment of the very quality of God and a world that has not. The former world, the one that I believe we live in, does not require periodic divine interventions to enable us, the creatures of such a world, to participate in God's own life. The relevant divine action in such a world is God's total and continuous gift to the world of this extraordinary potential – a property that could only have been bestowed by the God whose potency exceeds all ordinary conceptions of power. Perhaps this comes down to a matter of personal taste, but to my mind the gift of such a property to the world is a more wonderful and praiseworthy thing than anything envisaged by more 'interventionist' accounts of Incarnation and atonement. It is not, in fact, that I want to deny that the Incarnation can properly be understood as a divine action. But that 'action' is best understood as the special fulfilment of a potential that God has actively and continuously granted to be latent within the world from the beginning. It is more pleasing, I would suggest, to contemplate a piece of ebony, whose beautiful colour is a natural property arising from the intrinsic and long-evolved structure of the wood, than to settle for a piece of pine to which an 'ebony' dye has been applied, however convincingly. So it is, I think, with the Incarnation.

The question of divine intervention in the Incarnation can be transposed into a question about divine suffering on the Cross. If the Word's embodiment in the person of Jesus did not require a special divine intervention, perhaps Jesus' suffering on the Cross did not actually require God to suffer in God's-self. And if God did not suffer on the Cross, doesn't the Cross lose its redemptive and atoning power? My response would be to affirm that God did indeed suffer on the Cross. For if the Word was fully and perfectly embodied in Jesus, Jesus was in actuality – not just in appearance – the objective embodiment of God in the world. If Jesus' life and death fully and perfectly embodied the very quality of God, then an aspect of the quality embodied was the quality of God's suffering on behalf of the world. Anything that fully and perfectly embodies God's quality must be God. If this were not so then Jesus, by perfectly embodying the quality of God, would be another god besides God. The reason that is not the case, of course, is that Jesus embodies God's quality as God's incarnate Word. It follows, then, that Jesus' suffering on the Cross was God's suffering.

As with the question of the kind of divine action involved in the Incarnation, this view of divine suffering ought to enlarge our understanding of God's loving action towards the world, not reduce or narrow it. The suffering to which Jesus submitted himself on the Cross revealed (and was) the quality of God's suffering love for his creatures. This love – in the form of the potential for the incarnation of the full quality of God's being in the world – was latent within the created order from the beginning. God's suffering love is implicit in God's whole creative sustaining of the world; it is not something that came into play only in one gruesome historical event in the first century just outside Jerusalem. The Lamb, as Revelation 13: 8 puts it, "was slaughtered from the foundation of the world."

This, to return to the point of departure for the foregoing reflections, is why the embodiment and revelation of God's quality in the world is both an example of how God's love should be enacted and the objective realization and inauguration of God's Kingdom. When the Word is expressed and embodied in Jesus' life and death, the world is enabled to recognize and respond to the eternal nature of God's very being. Jesus' suffering on the Cross was the fulfilment of the revelatory potential that was granted to the created order from the beginning. By allowing himself to be horrifically scapegoated, Jesus expresses and actualizes God's eternal quality of siding with the victim. It is not that Jesus must be thought of as either the perfect illustration of God's love or as the decisive locus of action of that love. He was both. The semiotic model suggests that these two views, traditionally regarded as competing alternatives, are two equally real sides of the same coin.

※

It may be asked, finally, how the scapegoating theory of atonement might fit with a 'cosmic' Christology of the kind found in, say, the letters of Paul (or a follower of Paul) to the Colossians and the Ephesians. How does a scapegoating perspective on Jesus' life and death fit with the great Christological hymn of Colossians 1: 15-20, which declares that, "through him God was pleased to reconcile to himself *all things, whether on earth or in heaven*, by making peace through the blood of his cross" (my italics). Doesn't scapegoating sound like a vice that is quite specific to humans? If atonement through the Cross is simply God's way of rescuing us from this specifically earth-bound sin, what room is there for an account of the significance of Jesus' life, death and resurrection that has relevance to the whole of creation?

To attempt an answer to this question, let us extend our earlier analogy, based on the properties of ebony, a little further. There is a form of vulcanized rubber – that is, rubber that has been baked with sulphur in a controlled way – that is called 'ebonite'. It is so called because it looks and feels very similar to ebony wood.[3] Of course, this development of the analogy is rather inexact because the colour and other qualities of ebonite are not precisely the same as those of ebony wood. Nevertheless, I think you will see the point. Wood and vulcanized rubber are quite different material substrates but they can embody very similar qualities.

Might the same be true of the Incarnation? The Incarnation event that we recognize took place when – through a very specific set of religious, historical, biological and psychological circumstances – the world-stuff in our particular corner of the universe became formed into the person of Jesus. Might there be other combinations of circumstances, very different from those of Jesus of Nazareth, in which the fabric of the universe could come to fully and perfectly embody the quality of God? Could such circumstances arise on other planets, in other galaxies? Might they already have arisen? As Sydney Carter's carol puts it:

Every star shall sing a carol
Every creature high and low,
Come and praise the King of Heaven
By whatever name you know.

When the king of all creation
Had a cradle on the Earth,
Holy was the human body
And the day that gave him birth.

---

3 For a while ebonite was the material of choice for the manufacture of ten-pin bowling balls, which had previously been made from dense hardwoods. It is still used to make high-quality mouthpieces for some woodwind instruments.

Who can tell how many crosses,
Still to come or long ago,
Crucify the King of Heaven?
Holy is the name I know.

Who can tell what other cradle
High above the Milky Way
Still may rock the King of Heaven
On another Christmas Day?[4]

In that case, the quali-sign approach to the Incarnation would offer a way of thinking about Christology from a cosmic perspective. Wherever and however the quality of God's being is embodied in the fabric of the universe, creatures are offered the possibility of responding to, and reorientating their lives around, the incarnate Word. In doing so they would be turning towards, becoming partakers in, the very life of God.

Such a reorientation would always, we may reasonably suppose, result in a turning away from whatever structures and systems may have emerged that are contrary to God's nature and purposes. This may include tendencies to maintain complex societies of creatures by the psychological and physical mechanisms of scapegoating. It might also include redemption from other forms of sinfulness of which we have no experience on earth. The common factor would be that this redemptive turning point, wherever and whenever it occurred, would depend on the emergence within the created order of something that fully and perfectly embodies – that constitutes an iconic quali-sign of – the very being of God.

To what extent, then, might the scapegoating theory of atonement have cosmic relevance? I wonder whether the concept of creation *ex nihilo*, creation out of nothing, may be important here. This is the idea that God's creative activity occurs 'out of thin air', so to speak. Or rather, not out of thin air but out of nothing at all. This differs from creaturely ways of creating, which always make use of something that is already in existence.

The doctrine of creation *ex nihilo* is not found explicitly in the Bible, but became important in the early centuries of Christian thought as a way of distinguishing Christian thinking about the world from certain other views that were prevalent at the time. The concept of creation out of nothing served to affirm the absolute sovereignty of

4 Reproduced by kind permission of Stainer & Bell Ltd., London, England [www.stainer.co.uk].

God. If God created out of 'something', then that something must have existed alongside God from the beginning, in which case God does not have complete sovereignty over everything but has always had to share his 'space' with something else. The doctrine was also a way of affirming the goodness of the material world, contrasting with ideas of creation involving a hierarchy of intermediaries between God and matter, intermediaries who protected God from getting his hands dirty while he was creating.

The idea of creation out of nothing has come in for a certain amount of criticism recently for being allegedly abstract and unbiblical. I wonder, though, whether there may be a neglected aspect of the concept of creation *ex nihilo* that these criticisms overlook. Perhaps creation *ex nihilo* is not just a philosophical way of affirming the goodness of matter and the sovereignty of God. Might the concept also have a moral dimension: an affirmation that when God creates he never does so at the expense of anything or anyone else?

If God created out of something, rather than out of nothing, then that something would be used – or used up – in the process. That is what happens, in some form or another, in all creaturely acts of creation. Whether it is in the creation of a painting, which uses up canvas and pigment, or the creation of a society, which uses up human victims as scapegoats or treats them as disposable commodities, human creativity is never creation out of nothing. Admittedly, some kinds of creativity have less in the way of immediate material cost than others (painting less than sculpture, say, and musical composition less than painting). But the 'cost' of human creativity is never zero. In fact the history of the cosmos is a history of the emergence of some things at the cost of others. We are stardust: if stars didn't die, there would be no chemical elements from which human bodies could be made. If competition and death were not a feature of the biological world then there could be no evolution by natural selection. And if no evolution by natural selection, then no humans.

I'm prepared to bet that all complex creaturely communities will turn out to be sustained in one way or another at the expense of other creatures. Human scapegoating may only be a 'local' variant of this universal theme, but I suspect that atonement through the revelation and reversal of that theme may be a cosmic phenomenon. And further: perhaps in some sense atonement through the defeat of creation-by-victimization may be necessary for the redemption of the whole cosmos, a cosmos which, in its current form, at every level from Higgs bosons to human beings, derives its life at least in part from the dynamic of death and decay.

9

Holy, Catholic and Apostolic

Sunday by Sunday many of us are used to declaring our belief in
"one holy, catholic and apostolic church." What might this mean?
I suggest, based on the semiotic model, that these three 'marks'
(characteristics) of the church may be translated as declaring,
respectively, that the church is called to be transformative, truthful
and inclusive.

The reader may immediately suspect that a rather 'woolly
liberal' approach may be taken here. We shall see, however, that
affirming the church as transformative, truthful and inclusive has
a clearly God-centred (rather than liberal, human-centred) focus,
and, indeed, perhaps a rather radical edge. Furthermore, each of
these reinterpreted marks of the church will be found to correspond
to a different aspect of various advances in our understanding of
the Eucharist that have occurred during the last century or so. I
must emphasize that I do not intend this chapter to be taken as the
definitive conclusion to which the preceding ones have been leading.
Nevertheless, it seems appropriate to reflect a little on some possible
practical implications of the semiotic model of the Trinity.

Let us start, then, by asking what it might mean to say that the
church is holy. We might mean that it is pure, set apart from the
world. In some ways, that is surely true. But the semiotic model
suggests, further, that the church is the world in the process of
transformation; transformation, that is, into participation in the
divine life. The practical question for the church as it seeks to be holy
is, how can such a process of transformation be fostered?

I make no claim to have a universally applicable answer to this
question but I offer an example that may have some wider relevance.
For some time a small group of Methodists, Anglicans, Baptists and
others from our town have been meeting on Sunday evenings. We
follow a loose monthly cycle of Bible study, musical explorations,
prayer, meditation, and pastoral sharing and listening. Once a month
a minister from the Methodist circuit presides at a eucharistic meal.
The meal is prepared by members of the group and a conventional
eucharistic liturgy is woven into our ordinary eating and drinking.

The eucharistic rhythm has, to my mind, been central to the character of the group. While our range of views mirrors the diversity of the wider church, we have found in eucharistic fellowship with one another that our discussions have generally (though not invariably) led to growth rather than stalemate. Collectively, we have come to believe that this way of gathering is a genuine manifestation of 'church'. For some it has been a safe place while weathering difficulties in that person's congregation of origin. For others it has become, at least for the moment, their main or only continuing participation in the life of the body of Christ.

I do not suppose that this model of eucharistic fellowship is the solution to all the church's problems. Nevertheless, I think some general conclusions may be drawn from thinking about why, at least for a time, this particular model has worked for this particular group of people. First, the model contains the basic eucharistic structure that I have described in the preceding chapters. Specifically, it involves listening to and studying the Word, both in the form of Scripture and in the honest sharing with one another the reality of our own lives. Second, it involves a eucharistic response to the Word in the form of an ordinary meal, within which the sacrament instituted by Christ is celebrated. The meal, therefore, functions in the ordinary way of meals, bringing people around a table to engage in an everyday kind of giving and receiving. But it also (and because of this) works as a sacrament, being an interpretative response to the Word by means of which the participants are drawn individually and collectively into the very life of God.

When I'm out for a meal with friends or colleagues there is one thing – probably even ahead of the quality of the food or the atmosphere of the restaurant – that always seems to me to be crucial to the quality of the interactions. I'm thinking simply of the size and shape of the table. Too small and one is constantly wrestling for elbow room with one's neighbours. Too large and one is unable to converse comfortably with someone sitting opposite. I suggest that, in a metaphorical sense, the question for the church is, what is the shape of our tables? In other words, how well do our institutional structures and processes facilitate the kinds of fellowship that amount to a collective interpretative response to the Word as a true representation of the Father?

I need to emphasize that what I am saying is not primarily concerned with the size of the group. I am not arguing that 'small is beautiful'. What I am suggesting is that at every level and every unit of organization, the church must ask itself, "Are we making signs that properly represent and actualize the Kingdom?" If the answer is no, then we are not being the church. We are not being holy, and we are not being the locus of the world's transformative participation in the life of God.

❀

Of the several recent ecumenical convergences of liturgical thought and practice, the one that relates to the 'transformative' (holy) character of the church concerns the question of the 'real presence' of Christ at the Eucharist.

The key to understanding why the concept of real presence became such a contentious doctrinal issue for the church arguably lies in two developments that occurred in the first few centuries of Christianity.[1] In the earliest churches the Eucharist appears to have been celebrated alongside, or as part of, an ordinary meal, the *agape* (love) feast. After a while, perhaps for practical reasons, the eucharistic rite became separated from the ordinary meal. There would have been nothing wrong with that, providing that the eucharistic act had remained capable of enacting and embodying the kind of fellowship necessary for the actualization of the Kingdom. In other words, the Eucharist will 'work' as long as the sign itself (the meal, or schematized meal) actualizes what it represents (the Kingdom of God).

Unfortunately, what the church lacked was a sufficiently robust theology of signs to maintain the intrinsic connection between the eucharistic sign and the actualization of the Kingdom. For some time, the prevailing understanding of a 'symbol' (a sign, in our more precise semiotic terminology) had been a Platonic one, according to which the sign was understood to *participate* in some way in whatever it signified. This view of signs did not have the technical precision of modern semiotics, but it was nevertheless sufficient to underpin a sense that the eucharistic act as a whole was able (in the phrase that had not yet been explicitly formulated) to effect what it signified. The problems started when, in addition to the separation of the eucharistic rite from the *agape* meal, this understanding of the Eucharist as a sign that participates in what it signifies began to break down. Signs now came to be understood as things that merely stood in for other things without being directly connected with them or participating in their reality.

---

1 For this and my subsequent references to the history of eucharistic thought, see William R. Crockett, *Eucharist: Symbol of Transformation* (Collegeville, Minnesota: Liturgical Press, 1989).

The combined effect of these two developments – the separation of the Eucharist from the ordinary meal and the view of signs as having no intrinsic connection to the thing signified – was that it became unclear how the Eucharist could have any objective efficacy. In order to give an account of how the sacrament actualized the Kingdom, it therefore became necessary to suppose that something about the eucharistic sign was itself objectively changed in some hidden way into the reality that it signified. One way of achieving this was by holding that the words of institution during the eucharistic prayer caused a 'transubstantiation' of the ordinary bread and wine into the body and blood of Jesus, thereby actualizing the 'real presence' of Christ. From there it was a natural progression for the focus of the eucharistic liturgy to become the bread and the wine themselves and for special importance to attach to the priest who held the power to effect this change in their substance. The laity became reduced to mere observers of the process, encouraged to be absorbed in their private devotions until alerted that the time had come to witness the moment of consecration.

The Reformers, of course, reacted against this distortion of the eucharistic sign. However, since they likewise lacked an adequate theory of signification, they too had difficulty in resolving the problem. Martin Luther affirmed the real presence of Christ in the bread and wine while rejecting transubstantiation as the explanation of how this occurred. Ulrich Zwingli denied the real presence, arguing instead that Christ's presence was merely a matter of his remembrance by the congregation, a remembrance brought about by the direct action of the Spirit upon them. Thus Luther affirmed the real actualization of something in the Eucharist at the cost of narrowing this actualization to one moment of the rite. Zwingli retained a recognition of the holistic nature of the rite, but at the cost of denying any real transformation brought about specifically by the eucharistic sign.

The recent ecumenical convergence on the issue of the real presence of Christ at the Eucharist has involved an acknowledgement of the importance of the whole rite, instead of a focus on one particular moment within it. In addition, it is now widely recognized that, whether or not Christ is said to be really present in the bread and the wine, the sacrament is not effective unless received in faith by the communicant. In many Protestant liturgies, therefore, a deliberately ambiguous form of words is used, such as praying that the elements "may be to us" the body and blood of Christ. The overall effect of these developments is that the Eucharist is understood to be objectively effective in some way, bringing about a real transformation in the participants, while leaving the exact locus of that transformation open to different understandings.

It is sometimes said that this ecumenical accord on the question of the real presence of Christ has been possible because of a retrieval of the (originally Platonic) idea that signs can participate in the realities that they signify. That may be so. But I think the semiotic model is able to take us further. For, whereas current sacramental theology can only gesture towards a return to the pre-medieval understanding of 'symbols', the semiotic model offers a systematic account of signs, within which some signs are shown to have the property of causing to be actualized that which they signify. Moreover, the semiotic account is able to show how this can be true of ordinary things in the world (such as people gathered to share a meal) without resting on some mysterious, almost magical, understanding of a special kind of sign called a 'symbol'. Importantly, as I have been trying to show, the semiotic model also enables this understanding of the efficacy of the sacraments to be set within a coherent account of the relation of the church and sacraments to the Trinity and Incarnation.

The semiotic model suggests, in other words, a way of affirming (with Luther) the real transformative effect of the Eucharist and (with Zwingli) the holistic and communal basis of this transformation. In this respect, the semiotic approach can perhaps be understood as heir to a lineage traceable though Paul, Augustine and John Calvin. From the semiotic perspective, the real presence of Christ may be affirmed as being actualized within the whole church, the whole gathering of believers, as it hears the Word and makes an interpretative response to that Word as a true representation of the Father. If scriptural warrant for this view is required, it is found in Paul's understanding of the church as the body of Christ, and in Christ's own words: "For where two or three are gathered in my name, I am there among them" (Matthew 18: 20). This is not, as Zwingli held, a way of affirming the efficacy of the sacrament without attributing anything objectively effective to the material sign (that is, the whole eucharistic act) in itself. Rather, as Calvin recognized, following Augustine, the transformation of the church into the body of Christ occurs precisely because there is the strongest possible connection between the eucharistic sign and the reality signified.

In semiotic terms, then, the Eucharist functions to incorporate the community of believers into the representational life of God – the eternal activity of God's self-knowing in which the Word is interpreted by the Spirit as the true and perfect representation of the Father. The significance of the small ecumenical group to which I referred earlier may be understood in that light. The group has, in effect, re-connected the Eucharist with the *agape* feast from which it was separated very early in Christian history. The promise of this reconnection, I suggest, lies in the fact that such gatherings have the potential to allow Christians to experience the Eucharist actually functioning sacramentally as it ought to. It may be that if we, the church, were more often to return to using the scaffolding of an ordinary meal to support the Eucharist, we might find ourselves making more sense of the eucharistic rite on the other occasions when we celebrate it in abstraction from such a meal. Such a separation of Eucharist from ordinary meal might then turn out to be more liturgically sustainable than it has been until now. For we may hope, this time around, that the church may have learned how to avoid its understanding and practice of the Eucharist being distorted by its adherence to a deficient theology of signs.

❀

The church is 'holy' because it is transformative. Transformative not in some vague sense of general personal development, but in a specific and radical sense of being the locus of the world's incorporation into the eternal life of the triune God.

So what can we say about the second mark of the church? How, in light of the semiotic model, are we to understand the church's calling to be 'catholic'? What is it that gives the church its universal relevance and coherence, holding it together as one entity in spite of all its visible variations from time to time and place to place? I want to suggest that the church is catholic to the extent that it seeks to be truthful. And asking ourselves what being 'truthful' means in the context of semiotics will, I think, tell us something important about the nature of the church.

My reasons for suggesting that the universality of the church is a function of its truthfulness stem from the fact that truthfulness is a matter of rightful representation. The ultimate basis of the possibility of knowing anything at all is the fact that the Father is eternally represented by the Word. All worldly knowledge mirrors, in some way, this eternal act of truthful imaging. Creatures are able to participate in the divine life by themselves becoming interpreters of the Word as the perfect sign of the Father. The creature is thereby adopted into the place of the Spirit and transformed into a likeness of the Word. The church may then be understood as the 'place' in which creation is drawn into God's life. Since the church is constituted by its collective interpretative response to the one Word, it is one church.

The *unity* of the church rests, then, on the fact that the Word represents only *one* 'thing', the Father. Any part of creation that is being drawn into the divine life through its response to the Word is therefore part of this universally operative process. The church is 'catholic' because it is the world seeking to respond faithfully to the Word, the sign of the one Father, thereby being incorporated into the eternal being-and-knowing that is the life of God. Any truth-seeking that we undertake within the world must likewise be a reflection of the one ultimate source of truthfulness, God's eternal act of self-representation.

The Greek word in the New Testament that we translate as 'church' is *ekklesia*, which means the 'assembly'. Why, we may ask, can't individual creatures find their own way to the Father through the Word? Why do we have to 'assemble' to be the church? Part of the answer must be that all creaturely interpretations, as we have seen, are partial and fallible. No single creature is able fully to interpret the Word. We need one another in order to test and correct our interpretations, so that little by little our understanding may more closely approximate the truth. Clearly there is a parallel here with the collective nature of scientific inquiry. A difference is that, whereas science largely restricts itself to certain kinds of propositional knowledge, the church is meant to be the locus of the transformation of the totality of our being.

I fear that I am bound to be misunderstood on this point, so let me emphasize: I am not attempting to narrow the importance of the collective nature of the body of Christ to its function in securing an intellectual or propositional kind of knowledge of God. Rather, I am broadening the relation between representation and interpretation to include every possible dimension of our being. On this broadened view, 'knowing' the truth or 'speaking' the truth (by responding to the Word as the perfect representation of the Father) can be seen fully to happen only when we collectively exercise our various Spirit-dependent gifts, intellectual and otherwise (cf. 1 Corinthians 12: 1-11).

A related lesson from science about the nature of truthfulness is that true knowledge does not, and cannot, rest on secure 'foundations'. Again, this fact (which religious people often find extraordinarily worrying) follows from the nature of signs. If all knowledge depends on representing things with signs, and if all interpretations (thoughts, feelings or actions) made by finite creatures are potentially fallible, then all knowledge (at least creaturely knowledge) carries a degree of uncertainty. That is not to deny that we can make reliable claims to truthfulness – we can. What we can't do is show that those truth-claims are true *because* they rest on secure foundations.

If I may be allowed to introduce some philosophical terminology, what I'm saying is that our epistemology (our theory of knowledge) must be *non-foundationalist*. Let me illustrate the difference between foundationalist and non-foundationalist theories of knowledge with a well-known metaphor. Foundationalists hold that knowledge is like a great building, perhaps a skyscraper. The many levels of knowledge hold together because they build on the immovable support of the building's foundations. At first sight the building appears robust, but if the foundations are shaken the structure's vulnerability to collapse may suddenly become apparent. Moreover, once one part of the structure fails the rest is liable to follow.

In contrast, non-foundationalist knowledge has been compared to a ship at sea. The ship is reasonably seaworthy but imperfect. The advance of knowledge is like continuously rebuilding the ship while it is still afloat. Ultimately, every part of the ship may be in need of improvement but it cannot all be dismantled at once. The parts of the ship that are functioning well enough for the moment will be relied upon while we work on the structures that we suspect are the most deficient.

The church, I think, finds it difficult to accept that knowledge (even Christian knowledge) has no 'foundations'. I do not mean to say that Christian faith has no grounds, that there is nothing holding it together. The point, rather, is that its truthfulness does not depend on those grounds being demonstrably fixed and beyond doubt. As is well known, different parts of the church are inclined to locate the foundations of Christian knowledge in different places. Roman Catholicism claims that the teaching of the church is the main foundation, even to the point of being infallible. Some branches of Protestant thinking hold, instead, that Scripture is an infallible foundation of faith. Other strands of Christianity have claimed to find the bedrock of faith in either reason or experience, though both of these turn out to be a good deal more fallible than might initially be supposed.

All of these approaches, at least in their extreme forms, reflect a lack of trust in God's graciousness, a graciousness that is manifested in the gift of signs and sign-use as the means to creaturely incorporation in God's own life. The fear, I think, is that unless knowledge has secure foundations it cannot connect with the way things really are. The tragedy of the church stems at least partly from confusing *non-foundationalism* with *non-realism*. We worry that if knowledge does not derive its justification from resting on secure foundations, it can't claim to speak truthfully about reality. As a result we find ourselves, the church, scrabbling desperately for sources of certainty (ecclesial authority, Scripture, reason, experience) without realizing that in doing so we are shutting out the work of the Spirit.

The cure for this anxiety is to remember, as we saw at the end of Chapter 5, that knowing and being come together ultimately in the eternal triune life of God. As we are drawn into the life of God, either by directly interpreting the Word or in other forms of genuine truth-seeking, we participate in this convergence of knowing and being. Only if we doubt this will we feel the need to secure the truth by means of some other spurious foundation.

❀

What practical implications do these reflections on the nature of knowledge have for the church? The first thing to say is that desire for the truth should take priority over maintaining the unity of the church. Or rather, pursuit of the truth is the basis of the unity of the church, not the other way round. Attempts to safeguard the truth by shoring up the unity of the church will ultimately come to grief because the church's role is not that of protector of the truth – rather, the church is constituted by the truth.

This conclusion may have both institutional and 'grass-roots' implications. At the institutional level, it means that the church may undermine its own calling and integrity if it prioritizes immediate unity over the difficult process of honest pursuit of the truth. A church that seeks to base its unity on ecclesial authority is building itself into a house of cards. The more the authoritarian structure grows, the more catastrophic will be the eventual collapse. Of course, the relationship between institutional structure and the honest pursuit of the truth is not simple. To return to the analogy of science, the scientific community has its institutions and structures (academic bodies, learned societies, etc.) and the pursuit of scientific knowledge is facilitated by such structures. Even if these institutions are imperfect and sometimes resistant to new insights, nevertheless science would be harmed if they were dismantled at a stroke.

Similarly, with the church, when I say that truth must be the basis of the church's unity, not unity the basis of the church's truth, I do not mean to suggest that every little (or even medium-sized) disagreement should be the occasion for the dissolution of the church's institutional structures. Rather, I suggest that the church should be continually asking itself whether its present structures are those best suited to fostering the Spirit-empowered responsiveness to the Word that is the ultimate basis of its unity.

If working through the principle that seeking the truth is the basis of the church's catholicity is difficult at an institutional level, the implications at a 'grass-roots' level may be rather clearer. The church currently experiences enormous uncertainties about itself. In the face of divisions between and within our denominations, we are unsure how to deal with our differences. In the light of revelations about serious sexual abuses, for which we must take some collective ecclesial responsibility, we are unsure about how to restore our integrity and credibility. In the context of our 'post-Christian' secular era we are unsure how the church can authentically relate to society. With trends towards globalization and the diversification of communities, we are unsure how the church should relate to other faith traditions.

When science confronts areas of uncertainty and dispute it does not resolve its disagreements by means of top-down adjudication from its authorities and institutions. Rather, it empowers a diversity of research groups to investigate the matter in question in whatever ways seem most promising. Science as an institutional structure trusts that the surest way to the truth is from the bottom up. By analogy, I suggest that the role of the institutional church might be understood as that of equipping and empowering 'discipleship research groups'. That is, the church should aim to ensure that local eucharistic communities have access to the best current thinking and research, are offered the best models of working together and affirming one another, and are given genuine encouragement and permission to be seekers of the truth. Most of all, the wider church must trust that if the method of 'inquiry' is right, then the truth will eventually emerge.

The ecumenical development in eucharistic thought that especially corresponds to these reflections on truth and catholicity is the recovery of the Eucharist's pneumatological and eschatological dimension. That is to say, recent thinking about the Eucharist has recognized that the sacrament is future-oriented as much as backward-looking. It is about the anticipated heavenly banquet as much as about the meal Jesus shared with his disciples the night before his death. This reflects what we have seen about the nature of knowledge and the relation of knowledge to truth. We are engaged in a process of continually seeking the truth, our present state of knowledge being only ever a step on the way to understanding that truth. The truth draws us from the future rather than supporting us from the past. Creaturely knowledge will only correspond perfectly to the truth when all things are drawn into participation in the eternal life of perfect being-and-knowing that is the Trinity.

This is something, obviously, that can only be the subject of hope and anticipation. And this process of drawing us into knowledge of the truth is the work of the Spirit. Hence the importance of the *epiclesis* in the Eucharist, the calling-down of the Spirit on the bread and wine, on the gathered people, or on both. For it is by being adopted into the place of the Spirit that we become interpreters of the Word as a sign of the Father, and thereby participate in the eternal divine life of truthful representation.

In short, the catholicity of the church rests on trusting that it is the Spirit who will lead us to knowledge of the Father through the Son:

> When the Spirit of truth comes, he will guide you into all the truth, for he will not speak on his own, but will speak whatever he hears, and he will declare to you the things that are to come. (John 16: 13)

❁

The church, I have suggested, is holy to the extent that it is the locus of the world's transformative participation in the life of God. It is catholic to the extent that it makes a search for the truth (taking the broadest possible understanding of such truth-seeking) the basis of its unity and universality. In what sense, then, is it 'apostolic'?

One view is that the church is apostolic because her ministers have been ordained in an unbroken line stretching back to the apostles. For our purposes, however, I think it will be more helpful to take apostolic to mean something broader. I have in mind the understanding according to which to be apostolic is to be faithful to the witness of those apostles.

I suggested in the previous chapter that a central aspect of that witness was the recognition that Jesus exposed and disarmed the scapegoat mechanisms that so pervade our social interactions. In other words, the apostles witnessed to the fact that Jesus' whole life, death and resurrection was the ultimate undoing of the usual strategies through which, by means of excluding, blaming or victimizing others, groups and societies achieve their stability. In this, Jesus' ministry represented the fulfilment of a trajectory in Old Testament thought that had increasingly come to understand that God sides with the poor, the outcast and the stranger. I am saying, in other words, that the church is apostolic to the degree that it is radically inclusive.

To speak of the church's calling to be inclusive is not simply to say that everyone is welcome (though they are). Rather, it is to make the more specific claim that the church is called to constitute itself on some basis other than exclusion, blame or victimization. This may sound easy until we remember that the scapegoating mechanism only works by being hidden from view, below the consciousness of those (all of us) who are involved in it. Moreover, the mechanism is so ingrained in us that it is very difficult to be involved in any group (whether of friends, colleagues or co-worshippers) without some form of scapegoating beginning to operate. The point about inclusivity, therefore, is not primarily to do with the *scope* of the church (how far it reaches). The scope of the church is a function of its holiness and catholicity, a matter of how much of creation is drawn into the process of transformative, truth-seeking incorporation into the divine life. To say that the church is inclusive is, I think, to say something not so much about its scope but about its *mechanism of constitution*.

How can the church begin to ensure that it remains apostolic in this sense of avoiding scapegoating as the mechanism of its self-maintenance? Perhaps we should simply ask ourselves, who or what do we regard as the greatest threat to our continued functioning? Whom do we find ourselves most easily blaming for whatever difficulties we currently face? Of course, our answer to this question may turn out not to be completely mistaken. The scapegoat is not necessarily completely innocent, they are just not guilty of everything of which they are accused. But if we are inclined to blame our problems on, or feel particularly critical of, one particular person or group then there's a fair chance that something of the scapegoating mechanism is in play.

Having acknowledged whom we have cast in the role of our scapegoat, we should then take some tangible steps to ensure that we are not using our differences from this person or group to define and maintain our own identity. Suppose, for example, that our church tends to see children and young people as disruptive to our services. Our view of the ideal Eucharist is perhaps a quiet contemplative affair in which children, if present at all, are seen but not heard. If so, perhaps we should be asking ourselves, for example, why young children should not participate fully in the Eucharist, receiving the bread and wine alongside adults – perhaps even being involved in the distribution of the elements.

Of course, in other congregations it will not necessarily be children who are treated as the main scapegoats. Nevertheless, thinking about our attitudes to children in church may be a particularly good place to start, because how we treat children is such a clear sign of our willingness to accommodate those who are not like us. "Suffer the little children to come unto me, and forbid them not: for of such is the Kingdom of God" (Mark 10: 14, King James Version). More widely, however, my suggestion is that we can begin to check whether we are being truly apostolic by trying honestly to ask ourselves: "On whose outsider status does my feeling of being secure on the inside depend?" If there is any group of people whom we find ourselves collectively comfortable in aligning ourselves against, alarm bells should ring.

❀

The area of ecumenical convergence on the theology of the Eucharist that is relevant to these thoughts about apostolicity concerns the question of whether the Eucharist is a sacrifice. The debate on this usually takes it as a given that Jesus' death on the Cross was a sacrifice. The question then takes the form of asking whether the Eucharist in some way repeats this sacrifice (the tendency in some strands of the Roman Catholic tradition) or is merely a memorial of the sacrifice (a view emphasized in some Protestant thought). However, as we saw in the previous chapter, the scapegoating theory of atonement calls into question the whole nature of Jesus' self-sacrifice. According to the scapegoating approach, the efficacy of the Cross derives not from its effectiveness *as a sacrifice*, but from its power to reveal and dismantle the whole sacrificial structure of human social relationships.

On this view, any talk about the 'sacrifice' of the Cross must therefore be understood as if placed in inverted commas. It follows that when the language of 'sacrifice' is transferred to the Eucharist the same inverted commas should be retained, at least mentally. The scapegoating approach to atonement would be challenged if it turned out that the Eucharist is, after all, best understood in unqualified sacrificial terms. It is significant, then, that recent advances in our knowledge of early eucharistic liturgies have resulted in a more nuanced understanding of their 'sacrificial' character. Specifically, it has become clear that in the earliest traditions the bread and wine were often understood as being nourishing and life-giving rather than as the flesh and blood of a propitiatory sacrifice. The assembled people were thus offering themselves and their gifts as a thanksgiving for God's work in Jesus rather than as a re-enactment of a sacrificial killing.[2]

A related ecumenical convergence has been the recognition that the biblical and patristic use of the concept of anamnesis (a reference to the Eucharist as a memorial sacrament; "do this in remembrance of me") referred neither to an actual repetition of the event of the Cross, nor merely to a mental recollection of it. Rather, anamnesis may be understood as referring to the way in which the original event is made present in a form in which it becomes the basis of active participation in its redemptive reality.

The account I have given of the Eucharist as the model for, and locus of, our interpretative incorporation in the divine life is entirely consistent with these developments in liturgical understanding. There are implications, too, for our view of priestly ministry. According to one view, the principal role of the priest is to (re-)offer the eucharistic sacrifice on behalf of the people. Such a view loses its coherence if there is no actual sacrifice to offer. Nevertheless, the sacrificial view of priesthood may not be entirely wide of the mark. I say this because to offer a sacrifice is to make a sign. In the semiotic perspective, we might see the role of the priest as that of facilitating and co-ordinating the production of the sacramental signs that are central to the life of the church. We have seen earlier that the Eucharist is a rule-produced sign (as is baptism). The priest's role is to preside over the proper production of the sign. For, just as in the making of any other rule-produced sign, such as the formation of handwriting with a pencil or pen, if the signs are not properly produced they will be unintelligible.

This may appear to be rather a climb down from some 'higher' views of priestly ministry, in which the priest seems to be regarded as performing something close to magic in the administration of the sacraments. However, if we understand the sacraments as somehow constituting the church and forming us into the body of Christ, facilitating and presiding over the production of signs that

2 Paul F. Bradshaw and Maxwell E. Johnson, *The Eucharistic Liturgies: Their Evolution and Interpretation* (London: SPCK, 2012), pp. 19-24.

bring this about is a high calling indeed. Moreover, although the priest's presidency at the Eucharist is the paradigmatic example of his or her role in supervising the formation of the signs that actualize the Kingdom, their pastoral and other duties are likewise concerned ultimately with helping the people become shaped by the Spirit into a collective embodiment of the Word.

In short, the priest's work is to enable us to be formed (individually and collectively) into signs that actualize what they signify, where what is signified is the Kingdom of God. In translations of the New Testament it is the Greek word *mysterion*, or 'mystery', that came to be commonly translated by the Latin *sacramentum*. What makes the sacraments mysteries, though, is not that some magical or supernatural transformation takes place in the water, bread or wine that is used in the enactment of the sacramental sign. The 'mystery', it seems to me, is that the created order has been granted the capacity for the signs that can emerge within it to bridge the otherwise absolute divide that exists between creature and Creator. In a sense, it is this absolute otherness of God from the world, and the fact that by God's grace we may nevertheless come to participate in the divine life, which is the only thing that can properly be called a mystery.

And so we now turn, in Part III of the book, to consider the 'mystery of existence'.

Part III

The Mystery of Existence

10

Fingerprints of the Trinity

Fifteen years before the publication of Darwin's *On the Origin of Species*, an anonymous author caused a sensation in Victorian Britain by proposing an evolutionary view of biology. The author subsequently turned out to be an Edinburgh publisher called Robert Chambers; the title of his book was *Vestiges of the Natural History of Creation*.

I have sometimes wondered whether, slightly tongue-in-cheek, I should have given this book the same title. For mine is a book about creation, it is concerned with the natural emergence of certain aspects of living things (on which I shall say more in the next chapter), and one of its more original claims – to be explored here – has to do with 'vestiges' of a kind. I might add that, like Chambers in relation to biological science, I work somewhat on the margins of academic theology. My proposal, like the evolutionary theory presented in Chambers' *Vestiges of the Natural History of Creation*, may well be regarded with a degree of suspicion. Indeed, so hostile were the responses to the anonymous Scottish thinker's speculative scheme, fear of a similar reception was one of Darwin's reasons for delaying the publication of his own theory. But I console myself that Chambers did at least succeed in bringing the question of evolution to public attention, just as I would count it a success to get the semiotic perspective (back) on to the theological agenda. Furthermore, it may not be widely known that *Vestiges of the Natural History of Creation* consistently outsold *On the Origin of Species* well beyond the lifetimes of their respective authors!

Unlike Chambers, though, my interest is specifically in the idea of vestiges of the *Trinity* in creation. So what do I mean by 'vestiges'? In English, the word vestige often means something along the lines of a faint trace or remnant, as in the term 'vestigial organs' (such as the appendix). But the Latin, *vestigium*, can also mean a footprint – something much more direct and immediate than a mere trace or echo. It's this stronger sense of the term vestige that I would like you to consider as a way of thinking about the relation between the three-ness of God and the three-ness of the world. In fact, when I chose to call this book 'Traces of the Trinity' I did so with some reservations, for

I suspected that the word 'traces' would likely be taken to imply the weaker end of the spectrum of connotations of 'vestiges'. In contrast, it is my hunch that the three-ness of the structure of signs is not just a faint echo or dim reflection of the three-ness of the Trinity, but the direct imprint of the creative activity of God. Recently, for reasons I will return to, theologians have tended to be rather uncomfortable with the idea of trinitarian vestiges. I am going to suggest that, paradoxically, theological wariness of the concept may best be overcome by trying a bolder approach than the tradition has usually dared to endorse.

The starting point for our thinking about 'vestiges' is that there is a three-ness to the structure of signs, which seems to have a curious and perhaps unexpected resemblance to what Christian tradition has wanted to say about the 'structure' of the Trinity. Note that these parallels, which we explored in Part I, are what we might call 'non-trivial'. That is to say, it is not just that various aspects of the processes of signification seem to come in threes. Rather, there is a specific kind of three-ness – the three-ness of the elemental grounds of Quality, Otherness and Mediation – that keeps recurring throughout the structure of signs. It is this specific kind of three-ness that resonates with the traditional roles and relationships attributed to the Father, Son and Holy Spirit. So, when I speak of the three-ness of signs and the three-ness of the Trinity, I am using 'three-ness' as a shorthand for the very specific kind of three-ness to which we have been continually returning. I am not, in other words, merely succumbing to 'triadomania' – a pathological tendency to find triads in everything.

Let us consider the possible ways in which the three-ness of signs and the triune nature of God could be related. I suggest that there are three ways, which I am going to call analogies, likenesses and vestiges. These three options for construing the God–world relationship can be illustrated as in the diagram overleaf.

The first possibility is that the three-ness of the world offers a mere *analogy* for the three-ness of the Trinity. By this I mean that we have happened to notice a certain kind of three-ness in the world that we are now projecting on to God. Hence the direction of the arrow representing 'analogy' in the diagram is from the world back to God. In this scenario, our knowledge of the three-ness of God is represented as pale compared to our knowledge of the three-ness of the world.

Many theologians gravitate towards this weak kind of understanding of the link between our knowledge of the world and our knowledge of God, largely because they rightly want to affirm the utter transcendence of God. They would fear that claiming any real similarity between the three-ness of the world and the three-ness of God could imply the

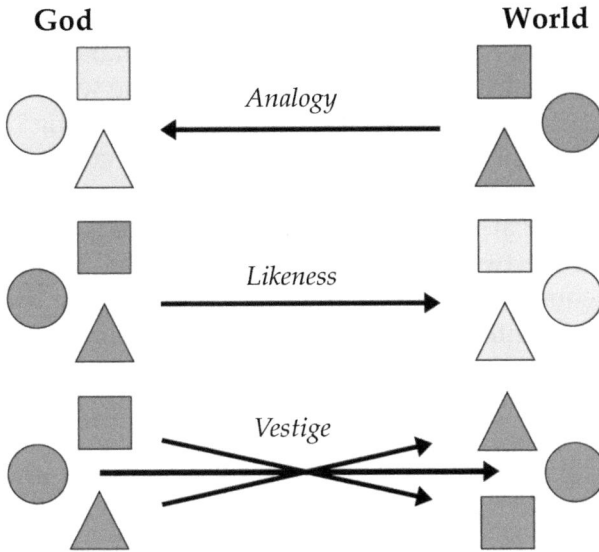

possibility of attaining knowledge of God that by-passes God's gracious self-revelation. In other words, there is a concern that if we claim that some feature of the world *really is* like the Trinity we imply that God exists on the same level as other things in the world. In that case, God might appear to be a being who can be compared to other created things, and this would be a lesser god than the God who is revealed entirely on his own terms as the transcendent Creator of everything.

This preference for the 'analogical' stance reflects an entirely legitimate theological concern. There is, however, a flaw in it. For, if the three-ness of the world does not truly reflect the three-ness of God, if it does not have its origin in God and yet we still want to affirm God's three-ness, there must be some kind of three-ness that the world and God *have in common*. If that is the case then the sovereignty of God is undermined after all, because God would be subject to description in terms of certain categories that apply to the world and to God *but do not originate with and in God*. This problem becomes ever more pressing the closer the apparent similarity between the analogy (in our case the elements of Quality, Otherness and Mediation) and what we have been led by other routes to say about God's 'inner' being.

Theologians are familiar with this problem in other forms. For example, they have sometimes wrestled with the following dilemma: Is loving others good because God *decides* that it is good, or does God want us to love others because it *is* good to do so? The problem here is that it seems odd to say that God could equally well have decided that it would be good for us to hate others. In that case, the goodness of love would appear to be rather arbitrary. But, if God wills us to love others *because* it is good to do so, the fact that love is good seems to be some kind of standard that would be true whether or not God wanted it to be. In that case, there is at least one thing (the goodness of love) over which God has no control, and that would make God less than the Creator of everything.

The theological resolution to this dilemma is to recognize that alongside these two options – that God either chooses that love is good or is constrained by the fact that it is – there is a third. The third option is articulated in Scripture, which says simply, "God is love" (1 John 4: 8). In other words, love isn't some external standard against which both the world and God can be measured. Love springs from God as something that is intrinsic to God's being.

The idea of the three-ness of God, I think, must be similar to that of God as love. Christians have found themselves compelled to speak of God in terms of a kind of three-ness. Certain aspects of the pattern of that supposed three-ness have quite an enduring character (e.g., Father as source, Son as Word, Spirit as mediator). Those patterns, I have tried to persuade you, seem curiously similar to the structures of signification and interpretation that have been uncovered by the philosophical field of semiotics. At first glance we appear to face the dilemma that either God chose to exist as a 'three-ness', as Trinity, or alternatively that the three-ness of the Trinity follows a pattern that originates outside God. The former would make the triune being of God appear arbitrary, the latter would undermine God's utter transcendence. The solution is to suppose that the three-ness of God is something that is intrinsic to God and that all other instances of such three-ness (such as the structure of signs) spring from God's being. In other words, God is 'three' in the same way that "God is love." The alternative is to say that three-ness has some kind of existence independent of God and the world, and that both God and the world can be compared to this ultimate model of three-ness in their different ways. But then God would not be God.

If I am right about the flaw in regarding all of our ways of picturing God as mere analogies, it makes sense to consider the possibility that at least some of the apparent resemblances between the world and God have a stronger basis. I am going to call this stronger view of the relationship a 'likeness'. A likeness, in the way that I'm using the term, would be a real similarity between God and the world.[1] Scripture

---

1 I make no claim that my use of the various key terms in the present discussion necessarily follows closely any of the established uses.

seems to have no particular problem with the idea that certain aspects of the world may genuinely resemble God. When it speaks of humans being made in the 'image' of God, it means that God intentionally made humans to be like God in some way. The alternative, as is well known, is that humans 'made' God in their own likeness (this might correspond with what I have been calling the 'analogy' view).

Note that in our diagram the arrow for 'likeness' therefore points from God to the world; the three-ness of the world has its origin in the three-ness of God. It is (as illustrated) perhaps a pale reflection of the divine three-ness, but it is nevertheless a *real* reflection of it. As such, the three-ness of the world can be understood as a true likeness of the three-ness of God without this undermining God's sovereignty and transcendence. That, indeed, is my guess: that God has graciously structured the world in such a way that the three-ness of Quality, Otherness and Mediation – the three-ness that underpins the structure of worldly signification – is a true likeness of the eternal dynamic of the Word's representation of the Father and the interpretation of the Word by the Spirit. In some ways this cannot be anything more than a guess, but it's a guess that I believe makes some theological sense.

❈

How does the idea of 'vestiges' of the Trinity fit with what I have said above about analogies and likenesses? The first thing to say is that if you examine the history of the idea of 'vestiges' in the Christian tradition I suspect you will find that what has generally been meant by vestige is roughly what I have been calling a likeness, or even something somewhat weaker. As we have already noted, Scripture does allow that God has intentionally created certain aspects of the world in his "image and likeness." But where the tradition has spoken of "vestiges of the Trinity" it has, I think, tended to mean something like a trace or echo of the triune being of God, an incidental resemblance rather than a deliberately imparted likeness. I shall leave historians to correct me on that if necessary. If I am right, the stronger meaning that I want to give to the 'vestige' concept would go beyond traditional theology. Paradoxically, though, given what I perceive to be a general theological aversion to the stronger end of the analogy–likeness–vestige spectrum, I think that the stronger version turns out to be more interesting and perhaps more theologically plausible.

Let us observe that there is a recurrent strand in the New Testament that speaks of the creation of the world as occurring through the Son/Word. The Word was with God in the beginning and all things came into being through him (John 1: 1-3); there is one Lord, Jesus Christ, through whom are all things and through whom we exist (1 Corinthians 8: 6); he is the exact imprint of God's very being, and he sustains things by his powerful word (Hebrews 1: 3); he is the image of the invisible God, . . . for in him all things in heaven and on earth were created, and in him all things hold together (Colossians 1: 15-17).

The Spirit is, of course, especially associated in the New Testament with the resurrection life, the new creation (e.g. Romans 8: 11), corresponding to her role as the animator of organic life in the Old Testament:

> When you hide your face, they [living things] are dismayed;
>> when you take away their breath,
>> they die and return to their dust.
> When you send forth your spirit, they are created;
>> and you renew the face of the ground. (Psalm 104: 29-30)

In fact, the idea of the 'trinitarian mediation' of creation has its roots in the Hebrew view that God created through his word, wisdom and spirit. Think, for example, of Genesis 1, where God's successive creative acts occur by means of his speaking (and God said . . .). Recall wisdom's role in creation in Proverbs 8: 22-31: "I was there when he drew a circle on the face of the deep . . . I was beside him like a master worker." And of course it was God's spirit (breath, wind) that swept over the waters right at the beginning (Genesis 1: 2).

We don't need to be held up here by questions of how and why these ideas about creation arose. It is enough for our purposes to note that such ideas have a firm place in Scripture and have subsequently maintained a significant role in Christian reflection on God's creative work. Irenaeus of Lyons (c. 130 – c. 200), to whom Christian thinking about creation owes a great deal, puts this in terms of creation taking place through the two "hands" of God, the Son and the Spirit.

To see how all this connects with what I want to say about vestiges of the Trinity, consider the following illustration. My wife enjoys making pottery. She isn't very interested in making pots on a wheel; rather, her creations are usually moulded by the direct actions of her fingers and thumbs. Imagine then, for the sake of argument, that she had made a pot on one surface of which something resembling the pattern of four fingers and a thumb could be clearly seen. What are the possible relations between this hand-like pattern and her actual fingers and thumbs?

One possibility is that the resemblance is entirely fortuitous. It just happens that the pot appears to carry something like a hand-print, but the similarity is entirely in the eye of the beholder. This possibility corresponds to the 'analogy' concept defined above.

A second possibility is that the resemblance to her hand is real and intentional but was not produced by the imprint of her hand. Rather, she sculpted a likeness of her fingers and thumb using the kinds of little wooden tool that I often find lying around the house. This option corresponds to my idea of a 'likeness'.

Finally, there is the possibility that the resemblance between the shape of the pot and the shape of my wife's hand was actually caused by the shape of her hand having been imprinted upon the pot. Of course, even then one might wonder whether this was deliberate or accidental, though I think she is a competent enough potter that the latter explanation could probably be discounted.

The logical possibilities for a Christian doctrine of creation are parallel, I suggest, to these imaginary scenarios from the work of a potter. I hope I have been able to persuade you that it is coherent and theologically plausible to hold that there is a real (as opposed to analogical) likeness between the three-ness of sign processes and the three-ness of God. And we have noted the traditional and scriptural view that God creates, in some sense, by means of this three-ness within his eternal being: the Father's creative activity is mediated by the agency of his two hands, the Word and the Spirit.

What, then, is the relation between the likeness we have identified (the three-ness of sign processes) and the way that likeness was created?

One possibility is that the likeness is real but the mode of creation has no direct relation to the likeness. This would correspond to my wife sculpting a likeness of her hand on the pot using her wooden tools rather than by the direct imprint of her fingers. Certainly this is an entirely defensible theological position, and perhaps God's dignity would in some sense be protected if we suppose that the action of his 'hands' is not directly discernible in the products of his creative work. But I confess that I find it more attractive to conjecture that the structure of the world, including the recurring threefold pattern that can be discerned within the structure of signs, reflects the direct and continuous creative work of the persons of the Trinity.

Let me spell out what I mean by this in relation to the element of Otherness. My suggestion is that every instance of Otherness in the world depends on and is somehow held in being by the Otherness that is the relation between the Father and the Son. In other words, the Word is the *creative ground* of all otherness in the world. This includes all the forms of otherness that we have seen within the various dimensions of the structure of signs. In the diagrams that I used in earlier chapters of the book to assist our analysis of the structure of signs, every square would represent a kind of otherness 'imprinted' on the structure of the world by the grounding Otherness of the Word. For example, the otherness of signs from their objects may be understood as a manifestation of this element of Otherness that the Word imprints on, and opens up within, the created order. And, as we have seen, the element of Otherness recurs at other levels and dimensions of the structure of signs. At each of these levels and dimensions, I am suggesting that the particular forms of otherness that we discern in the world are 'vestiges' of – they bear the imprint of – the creative activity of the Word.[2]

In the same way, I would see every instance of Mediation in the world as depending on and being held in being by the creative work of the Spirit, the mediator between the Father and the Son. In other words the Spirit is the creative ground of all mediation in the world. Within the structure of signs, for example, every occurrence of a triangle in our earlier diagrams can be taken to reflect a form of mediation 'imprinted' on the structure of the world by the creative grounding of the Spirit. When a sign comes to mediate between an object and an interpreting agent, this mediation may be understood to be made possible by a certain kind of 'structure' that the eternally mediating Spirit imprints on, and opens up within, the created order. The same goes for all of the other manifestations of Mediation we have identified within the structure of signs.[3]

It is important to emphasize that what the creative work of the Word and Spirit imprint on the world when they are acting as the two 'hands' of God is a 'structural pattern', not the specific content with which worldly processes 'fill' that structure. Perhaps the

---

2 The Word is therefore the creative ground of the otherness of sign from object, of the otherness of indexes from the causes of those indexes, of the otherness of stand-alone signs from all that is not significant in the background, and of the otherness that is brought to bear when signs are interpreted by actions.

3 We may therefore understand the Spirit as the creative ground of the mediation of the sign between object and interpreting agent, of the different kinds of mediation involved in the rules that connect symbols to their objects, of the mediating rules that determine the production of rule-produced signs, and of the mediation involved when signs are interpreted by thoughts.

following somewhat inadequate analogy may help to make this point. Suppose that the situation before God created anything is represented by a blank page. The blankness of the page represents the 'nothing' from which God creates *ex nihilo*. (Already the analogy is problematic, because the nothing may appear to be 'something'.) Now suppose that a grid of faint dots is imprinted onto the page. The dots represent the possibility of Otherness, which is imparted to the world by the creative work of the Word. So far the grid does not represent anything actual within the world; it is merely a 'structure' within which actual instances of Otherness can arise.

Now imagine that some (not all) of the dots turn from faint to bold. The bold dots are the actual instances of Otherness that emerge within the world, each bold dot representing something that is other than its closest neighbouring bold dots. So far there is nothing connecting the bold dots so there is no intelligible pattern, just meaningless differences and oppositions. Now suppose that some (but not all) of the bold dots become joined up by lines. This is brought about – or rather, made possible – by the creative work of the Spirit, which imprints on the world the possibility of mediation and continuity. If the world lacked this 'vestige' of the eternal mediating activity of the Spirit it would never have had the capacity to develop patterns and meanings, including the patterns and meanings that arise from the various levels and dimensions of signs.

On this analogy, the creative work of the Word and Spirit gives rise to a structure of the created order that enables the world freely to develop a 'dot-to-dot' picture of its own making. The existence of the dots and connecting lines is grounded in the work of the two hands of God; the actual 'picture' that emerges is a reflection of the freedom that God has granted to the world. At every moment of the world's existence, however, the underlying patterns of Otherness and Mediation are absolutely dependent upon the ongoing creative activities of Word and Spirit.

One of the dangers of this analogy is that it might be taken too literally. I'm not saying that the world is actually a dot-to-dot picture. What I'm trying to convey is the way in which every kind of Otherness and Mediation in the world is a vestige of, or bears the imprint of, the creative work of the Son and Spirit. With that caution in mind we can add to the dot-to-dot analogy the aspect of the created order that is a vestige of the eternal being of the Father. Having joined the dots of the picture, it can now be 'coloured in'. The colours are analogous to the qualities that emerge from within the world's structures of Otherness and Mediation. It is not that the Father does the colouring, or even that he defines the palette of colours from which the world chooses. Rather, the Father is the ground of the possibility of any colours (qualities) emerging at all. Some of the qualities that emerge within the world may be opposed to, and incompatible with, the quality of God's love. Again, this is a reflection of the freedom that God grants to the world. But crucially, our earlier reflections on the Incarnation lead us to affirm that the world has been granted a capacity for God-like qualities to emerge within it, even the very quality of God's love itself.

As with vestiges of the Word and Spirit, then, we may say that every instance of Quality in the world depends on, and is grounded in, the Quality that is God the Father. This would include every kind of quality, or 'in-itself-ness', within the structure of signs, such as the quality of the object-in-itself, or of the sign-in-itself. In our earlier diagrams, every occurrence of a circle would likewise represent the possibility of Quality 'imprinted' on the structure of the world by the grounding Quality of the Father.[4]

There is an intentional overlap in terminology here, in that from the outset I gave the collective name of 'elemental grounds' to the triad of Quality, Otherness and Mediation. I am now saying that the Father, Son and Spirit are the 'creative grounds' of these 'elemental grounds'. This overlap is appropriate because in each case the idea of a 'ground' has a similar sort of meaning. In the world, Quality, Otherness and Mediation are the basis of – the ground of – all particular instances of quality, difference and connectedness. But those 'elements' in the world exist by virtue of having been created by (or, which comes to the same thing, by being continuously held in being by) their corresponding 'creative grounds', the Father, Son and Spirit. In the part of the diagram near the beginning of this chapter which represents the 'vestiges' option (p. 119), each of these kinds of direct and continuous creative work of the persons of the Trinity is represented by an individual arrow between the trinitarian person and the corresponding element in the world.

For the moment, I have not said anything about how all three persons of the Trinity work inseparably together: we will turn to that question in Chapter 13. However, it is important to see here that, just as the Word and Spirit impart a structure to the world, their specific kinds of creative work also shape the pattern of God's

---

4   The Father is thus the creative ground of the quality, in itself, of the object represented by the sign, of the in-itself-ness of the sign-in-itself, of the quality that relates any particular iconic sign to its object, of the quality that is itself the sign in a quali-sign, and of the quality, or in-itself-ness, of the feeling that constitutes an emotional form of interpretation.

overall relation to the world. The Word is other than the Father, and this Otherness is the basis of the world's otherness from God. The world can only be distinct from God – creation rather than Creator – because within the Creator there is an eternal (uncreated) distinction between the Father and the Son. Note that the distinction between Father and Son is a distinction within the eternal being of God and so does not imply any inequality in their level of being. But this eternal Otherness is the basis of the absolute otherness of the world from God. The work of the Word in this regard is to give the world its freedom to be itself. Of course that freedom must be, in some sense, the reason behind the possibility of evil and suffering within the world. Whatever one wishes to say about how a good God can allow suffering (which I shall say a little more about in Chapter 12), a fundamental point must be the Otherness that has been given to the world through the creative work of the Word.

If there was nothing more to say about the world's relation to God than its Otherness, we would be thinking of a world that could have no continuing relationship with its Creator. It is the work of the Spirit to mediate between God and the world. Everything discussed in previous chapters about the world's participation in God through the medium of signs depends on acknowledging the possibility of some kind of mediation that can bridge the otherwise infinite abyss between Creator and creation. Without such mediation we would have a world of signs that operated without any possible connection between those signs and God's eternal life of self-representation. That signs have the capacity to mediate between the world and God – paradigmatically, as we have seen, in the sacraments – is a function of the creative work of the Spirit.

❁

I am offering, then, a strong version of the concept of 'vestiges of the Trinity'; indeed, as I have acknowledged, it is a stronger view than the theological tradition has normally wished to entertain. One of the attractive things about the concept is that it offers a way of affirming both the absolute transcendence and the radical immanence of God in creation. Many theologies of creation end up emphasizing one of these at the expense of the other. If we concentrate on upholding God's absolute difference from and transcendence over the world, we run the risk of failing to know God as the one who is closer to me than I am to myself, as Augustine put it. On the other hand, if we focus on God's immanence and involvement in creation, we may find it difficult to articulate how God is 'totally other' than the created order.

In the account that I have been trying to outline here, the absolute otherness of God from creation is fully affirmed. Indeed, Otherness is understood as one of the fundamental features of reality, a feature that originates within the very being of God. The otherness between the world and God must be grounded in the eternal Otherness within the Trinity. The God–world otherness is different in kind, not just in degree, to the innumerable instances of otherness within the world. The otherness between God and the world is the otherness of Creator from creation; the latter depends absolutely and at every instant of its being on the former. It is an *Other kind of otherness*. And yet, the manner in which this absolute otherness and dependence is upheld is a mode of creation that could not be more immanent or intimate. The very structures of the world, the elements of Quality, Otherness and Mediation that make signification possible (and thereby underpin personal existence), are held in being – moment to moment – by the direct and continuous creative action of the trinitarian persons themselves, Father, Son and Holy Spirit.

In short, the best way of constructing a theology of creation that does justice to God's transcendence (and immanence) is not, I think, to underplay the human capacity for knowledge of God. Rather, it is robustly to affirm that all such capacities depend absolutely on God structuring the world in such a way that creaturely knowledge is possible. Such a theology can be made coherent by recognizing that our worldly structures of signification are directly and continuously grounded in the eternal dance of meaning that is the very life of the Trinity.

I must emphasize that, in inviting you to consider this strong version of the vestiges concept, I am not claiming to be able to prove any of what I am saying, nor would I wish to try to do so. All I can say is that I think the standard theological objections to the stronger end of the spectrum of possible kinds of God–world relation are understandable but misguided.[5] If all I can do is persuade you that the three-ness of the world is a likeness (not a mere analogy) of the three-ness of God, I will be reasonably happy. I say this because I think that the idea of real 'likenesses' is a coherent theological position, one that enables us to make some sense of the relation between God and the world by means of reflection on the structure of signs. I wonder whether, further than that, I may have tempted you to consider that the everyday manifestations of Quality, Otherness and Mediation that characterize our moment-to-moment experience might genuinely be vestiges of the Trinity in creation.

---

5 I shall pick up this point in a different way in Chapter 12.

11

Life in the Semiotic Matrix

You probably know the joke about the drunk who is looking for his lost keys under a lamppost. When asked whether that is where he dropped them he replies, "No, but this is where the light's best."

In this chapter I want to highlight two areas of science in which most research has arguably amounted to looking mainly where the light is best. I have in mind the field of origin-of-life research and the study of human evolution. In each case I want to ask whether a semiotic perspective might offer much-needed illumination of these shadowy areas of scientific inquiry. If it does, there would be some important theological implications.

In 1953 the biosciences were transformed almost overnight by the discovery of the structure of DNA, the basis of the genetic code. Not surprisingly, the implications of this discovery have helped to shape the kinds of questions that tend to be asked by those investigating the origin of life. Scientists want to know how the basic building blocks for molecules such as DNA, and the closely related RNA, could have arisen from a primordial chemical soup. Moreover, the structure of DNA (and RNA) leads to a very neat mechanism whereby these kinds of molecule can act as templates for their own replication. As James Watson and Francis Crick observed in their famous paper, "It has not escaped our notice that the [structure] we have postulated immediately suggests a possible copying mechanism for the genetic material."[1]

In ordinary biological processes in present-day organisms, accurate replication of these kinds of molecule requires much additional chemical machinery. This machinery is present in complex biological cells, but would not have been available to life at its beginnings. Nevertheless, it is possible that the template-like structure of DNA and RNA may offer an important clue about how self-replication first started. Origin of life research has, not unreasonably, invested a lot of energy in investigating the origins of the replication of these molecules. I wonder, though, whether

---

1 J.D. Watson and F.H.C. Crick, 'A Structure for Deoxyribose Nucleic Acid,' *Nature*, vol. 171 (25 April 1953), pp. 737-738.

scientists have become rather too easily seduced by the elegance of these replicative mechanisms and the experimental possibilities they open up. Might the technologies available for investigating genes and genomes be the tempting pool of light under the lamppost, the easiest place to concentrate the search? Illuminating as the properties of these wonderful molecules may be, unless we know what life *is* we don't really know whether this is the best place to start looking.

Do we know what life is? You may, like me, have had to learn a list of the characteristics of life at school: things like self-maintenance, growth, metabolism, adaptation, response to stimuli, reproduction. But this is a descriptive list rather than a precise specification. The fact is that, although we generally have no difficulty in telling whether something is alive, we find it much more difficult to define life – to say what exactly distinguishes the living from the non-living. And if we cannot do that, how would we know where to look for clues about life's origins?

Throughout this book I have invited you to think of signs and sign-processes as somehow essential to our ordinary existence and yet almost invisible to us in our everyday lives. What if this 'blindness' to signs is also clouding our understanding of what constitutes being alive? Is it possible that the standard lists of the characteristics of living things miss out something fundamental? Could a crucial aspect of life be a capacity to interpret signs?

Consider an amoeba – a single-celled, blob-like organism which crawls around eating bacteria. The amoeba doesn't rely on pure chance to find its next meal. Instead it detects chemical traces of its bacterial prey and follows those traces until it finds their source. The amoeba, in other words, interprets the presence of certain kinds of molecule as a sign that there is a bacterium – a potential meal – in the vicinity. In semiotic terms the bacterium is the object, the attractant molecule is the sign of that object, and the amoeba is the agent that makes an interpretative response to the sign.

Thinking further about the kind of sign–object relation involved here, the molecule is an *indexical* sign of the bacterium. This is because there is a direct relation of cause and effect between the presence of the bacterium and the presence of the attractant molecule. The molecule is there because it has been released by the bacterium (though obviously not because the bacterium wishes to be detected by an amoeba). We can also see that of the three possible kinds of interpretation (feelings, thoughts and actions) the amoeba's response to the chemical attractant is an action. The amoeba responds to the sign by making movements in the direction of the chemical gradient of attractant molecules. This may turn out to be a *misinterpretation* in the sense that the amoeba may respond to molecules that are not, on this particular occasion, signs of the presence of the right kind of bacterium. If the chemical, or something like it, causes the amoeba to start chasing food that is not there, the amoeba will incur a cost for its misinterpretation, using precious energy to no avail.

The amoeba's response to the chemical gradient therefore shows all the features of interpretation that we have met in previous chapters. It is a response to a sign, the sign in some way stands for an 'object', and the interpretation is fallible in that, in any particular instance, it may not lead to the intended outcome. Perhaps, then, it would be useful for origin of life researchers to ask, what is the simplest kind of entity or organism that could have this kind of capacity for interpreting signs in its environment? Are there cellular structures simpler than an amoeba that could do this? Could an entity even simpler than a cell – perhaps something as simple as a single molecule – make a useful interpretative response? My colleague Christopher Southgate and I have attempted, with some success, to interest origin-of-life researchers in looking in this direction instead of under the usual lampposts. We are privileged to have been collaborating with biochemist Niles Lehman on a project to investigate whether RNA molecules may be capable of developing interpretative behaviour of a primitive kind.[2] If you are interested in pursuing our philosophical and scientific investigations I shall have to direct you to our more technical articles.[3] For the moment, for

---

2 RNA (ribonucleic acid) is a type of molecule that may have been important in the origin of life. Like DNA, its structure lends itself to storing and replicating 'information' and, like proteins (but unlike DNA) it is also able to facilitate (catalyse) reactions involving other RNA molecules. This has led to the concept of an 'RNA world': a system of RNA molecules from which life-like properties might have emerged before DNA and proteins existed.

3 Andrew Robinson and Christopher Southgate, 'A General Definition of Interpretation and its Application to Origin of Life Research', *Biology and Philosophy*, vol. 25, no. 2 (March 2010), pp. 163-181; Leong Ting Lui, Z. Ron Yang, Andrew J.N. Robinson, and Christopher C.B. Southgate, 'Interpretation and the Origin of Life', *Biological Theory*, vol. 5, no. 2 (Spring 2010), pp. 112-116; Niles Lehman, Andrew Robinson and Christopher Southgate, 'Empirical Demonstration of Interpretative Behaviour in Catalytic RNA', paper presented at Origins 2014, the second joint international conference of ISSOL (the International Astrobiology Society) and Bioastronomy (Commission 51 of the International Astronomical Union), Nara, Japan, 10 July 2014; further publication of our work on interpretation in RNA systems to follow.

the sake of argument, let's suppose that there does turn out to be something in this way of looking at the origin-of-life problem. That's all very interesting, you may say, but from a religious or theological standpoint, so what?

The theological importance, I think, is that it would mean that the same basic structures of signification and interpretation would have been shown to connect all living things. The earth is about 4.5 billion years old and life first emerged here about 3.8 billion years ago. Such lengths of time are unimaginably large compared with the sorts of timescale we can normally get our heads around. I find it useful to think about the evolutionary narrative in terms of a 450-page book. Even with such a thick volume, the history of the earth would have to be squeezed in at a rate of 10 million years per page. On this analogy, life appears on page 70, but modern humans don't make their appearance until the very last line of page 450. And the period from the patriarch Abraham in the book of Genesis until the present day (about 4,000 years, say) would take up the very last letter of this last line of the book.

Against such a backdrop what can we possibly say about human significance, dwarfed as we are against the long horizon of life's meandering history? And what was God up to during the eras and aeons before humanity emerged? If we think about life in terms of signs and interpretations, we may begin to see the shape of some kind of answer. For, according to the 'biosemiotic' approach, the human capacity for using signs is not an isolated event, only appearing in the last few 'words' of a long and otherwise meaningless story. Rather, human sign-use would be seen to be in continuity with the whole history of life. Certainly, as we shall explore shortly, there may be something special about the human capacity for signification and interpretation. But our special semiotic capabilities are embedded within, and arise out of, the much larger context of life's long history of recognizing, interpreting, and making signs.

On this view we may say, with Jesper Hoffmeyer, that biological evolution has been an exploration of the possibilities of 'semiotic freedom'.[4] Different organisms have different capacities for making and using signs. The earliest and simplest living things may have been able to interpret their environments in very basic ways, as suggested above. As living things became more complex and sophisticated, they became increasingly adept at making sense of

---

4 Jesper Hoffmeyer, *Signs of Meaning in the Universe* (Bloomington and Indianapolis: Indiana University Press, 1996), p. 61.

their environments. This involved not only interpretation of their external environments, but also of their internal environments. The latter kind of interpretation is the basis of homeostasis, the organism's capacity to regulate its internal systems. Organisms also began to use various forms of 'internal' self-representation. This job of internal representation is what DNA is doing when it functions as a 'code'. The sequence of nucleotide building blocks of the DNA molecule spells out, in three-letter words, the sequence of amino acids that must be strung together to make a functioning protein.[5]

Some organisms developed capacities for making signs in order to communicate with their fellows. Think, for example, of the pheromones released by ants, which control the behaviour of the whole colony. Even simple organisms such as bacteria are capable of forms of chemical communication with one another. Signalling can also take place between individuals of different species, as in the 'convention' that has evolved according to which yellow and black stripes signify that the organism is toxic. In a twist on this, some insects have evolved a similar kind of signalling as a devious form of defence mechanism, mimicking their noxious cousins even though they are not themselves harmful to predators.

If we were to trace this growth of semiotic freedom down all the branches and twigs of the evolutionary tree, we would no doubt find an enormously complex interplay of the various sign-types that we have examined earlier in the book. We would find icons, indexes and symbols; we would find quali-signs, stand-alone signs and rule-produced signs. And we would find, first, interpretative actions (like the change in direction of the amoeba's crawling), later perhaps interpretative feelings (though we don't currently know when anything that could be called a feeling emerged) and eventually interpretative thoughts. I don't think this semiotic map of biological evolution would necessarily show any straightforward

---

5 Proteins consist of chains of amino acids. The order of the amino acids in the chain determines the shape of the protein molecule when the chain folds up on itself, and this shape determines the protein's properties and biological functions. DNA consists of sequences of building blocks called nucleotides. There are four different nucleotides in DNA, usually designated by the symbols A, G, C and T. The 'words' of the DNA sequence consist of triplets of nucleotides. For example, the triplet CAG codes for the amino acid glutamine. In this way the whole sequence of amino acids in a protein is specified by a series of triplet 'words' in the corresponding section of DNA.

progression of sign-types from 'lower' to 'higher' forms of semiosis. In fact (as we shall see below) there might be theological as well as scientific reasons to expect otherwise. But I do think there would be a general increase in the complexity and multi-layered character of biological signification. The patterns of semiosis would be seen to be becoming richer, more 'colourful', and finer grained as life evolved from proto-biotic entities, through single-celled to multi-cellular organisms, and eventually to sophisticated sign-users like us.

As we have seen, the kaleidoscopic patterns of semiosis, which I am now suggesting at least partly explain the growth of biological complexity, depend on the operation of all three of the elemental grounds. But of these, Mediation may be said to have a particularly distinctive and essential role in the emergence of life. It is the element of Mediation that allows something to act as a sign – to mediate between the object and the interpreting entity. Without the operation of the elemental ground of Mediation the world would never have progressed beyond mere 'billiard ball' dynamics: there would be nothing more interesting than inanimate cause and effect, push and pull, action and reaction. Without mediation there would be no meaning. And without meaning (in the sense of signification), nothing would be alive.

Mediation, as we saw in Chapter 2, is the particular characteristic and gift of the Spirit. In Scripture there are two apparently contrasting traditions concerning the Spirit's activity. On the one hand, the Spirit is the source of the ordinary life of every living thing. Think, for example, of the picture of life breathed into all living creatures in Psalm 104 (vv. 24-30), from which I quoted earlier. In the context of a biosemiotic perspective we can affirm, in line with this strand of tradition, that living things are rightly understood to be animated by spirit. For signification, based on the Spirit's work of mediation, is what must be breathed into inanimate matter to bring it to life. On the other hand, and in apparent contrast, there is the tradition according to which the Spirit is thought of as the source of specific gifts granted variously to different human individuals. But note how many of the gifts of the Spirit in 1 Corinthians 12 have an implicitly semiotic character: utterance of wisdom, utterance of knowledge, prophecy, discernment, tongues and the interpretation of tongues. There is a deep connection, then, between being alive in the sense of being a living creature and being alive in the sense of being individually and specially inspired.

Mediation (grounded in the Spirit) is the basis of every kind of signification, from the processes of representation and interpretation which are essential to the simplest and most basic biological processes, to those that lie behind the most varied and individual instances of human insight and creativity. The common factor is the Spirit's gift of allowing signs to mediate between an agent (interpreter) and the object for which the sign is thereby enabled to stand. So it makes sense to affirm – as we do in the 'Nicene' Creed – that the Holy Spirit is "the Lord, the giver of life."

❀

If the simplest living thing is the simplest entity capable of making the most primitive kind of interpretation, what is the 'highest' form of signification and interpretation? One view is that what makes humans distinctive is the way in which we, alone among animals, have learned to use symbols. Only humans make use of complex languages in which the words (signs) mostly relate to their objects purely by convention. It is this arbitrary relationship between words and things that makes language so flexible and powerful. But it also makes fully fledged language use almost impossible even for our closest evolutionary relatives, the great apes. Terrence Deacon has, with good reason, called us "the symbolic species."[6]

This, I am sure, is indeed part of the answer to the question of human distinctiveness. Indeed, by introducing semiotic questions into the investigation of human evolution, Deacon has pointed evolutionary theorists into some previously un-illuminated territory. For example, if what makes humans distinct is a capacity to use symbols (in the technical sense of signs that are related to their objects by convention), then we may ask what sorts of brain structure and organization are necessary for this kind of capability, and why other animals (even our closest primate relatives) find it so hard to get the knack of learning a language.

But perhaps symbols are not the whole story. In the years following his voyage on HMS *Beagle*, Darwin recorded his ruminations on evolution in a series of small notebooks. On page 36 of *Notebook B* (1837-8) there is a famous diagram. The sketch looks like a rather spiky tree. At the ends of some of the branches Darwin added the letters (symbols) A, B, C and D. His scrawled notes underneath indicate that these represent different species of varying degrees of relatedness. At the top of the page he wrote, "I think."

Darwin's diagram, then, was a form of thinking. But what kind of thinking? The interesting thing, I suggest, is that Darwin was not

6 Terrence W. Deacon, *The Symbolic Species: The Co-evolution of Language and the Brain* (New York and London: Norton, 1997).

thinking purely symbolically, but iconically. He was imagining the relationship between species to be *like* a branching tree. You will recall that a sign based on a likeness is an icon, not a symbol. So Darwin's diagram involves both iconic elements (the branching tree) and symbols (the capital letters signifying the particular species represented by the branches).

Perhaps this example might suggest that the distinctiveness of human cognition lies not merely in our capacity to use symbols, but also in our having learned the trick of creatively combining symbols with other sign-types, especially icons. The idea that something other than purely symbolic thought was involved in certain great scientific advances is not new. A famous example is the way in which August Kekulé allegedly hit upon the ring structure of benzene during a fireside reverie. When Kekulé imagined a snake swallowing its tail his dream opened up a whole new field, that of organic chemistry. Similarly, Einstein is said to have discovered the theory of special relativity when, while travelling to his job at the patent office in Bern, he imagined what would happen if the bus were able to move away from a familiar clock tower at close to the speed of light. By means of this thought-experiment he realized that the passage of time is not fixed but depends on one's speed relative to other things.

Various attempts have been made to give some sort of theoretical basis for the importance of imagination in human cognition. Arthur Koestler called this kind of process 'bisociation', by which he meant the mental operation of bringing together two apparently unrelated 'planes' of thought. More recently a movement in cognitive psychology has developed the concept of 'conceptual blending'.[7] What semiotics adds is the insight that what lies at the heart of these various ways of understanding human creativity is the power of iconic signs to open up new windows on reality. Icons enable us to recognize previously hidden similarities between things: the structure of benzene made thinkable by means of the image of a snake swallowing its tail, the relationships between biological species made thinkable by Darwin's tree-like diagram. The recognition of iconic similarities such as these can lead to new, previously inaccessible ways of understanding the world.

This may be all very interesting for understanding certain episodes in the history of science, but does it tell us anything more generally

---

7 Arthur Koestler, *The Act of Creation* (New York: Macmillan, 1964); Gilles Fauconnier and Mark Turner, *The Way We Think: Conceptual Blending and the Mind's Hidden Complexities* (New York: Basic Books, 2002).

about ourselves and our relation to the world and to God? I think it does, for the reason that it gives us a different way of thinking about the question of the 'highest' form of signification. If we think that symbolic signs are the most sophisticated and powerful form of representation, we may be tempted to think that signs have a hierarchical kind of relation to one another. Perhaps we will think that icons are the simplest kind of sign, involving mere resemblances; that indexes are an intermediate kind of sign, affording knowledge of the hard facts of reality; and that symbols give us access to a whole new realm, a realm that opens up when our signs are freed from the constraints of being tied (by resemblance or causal connection) to the world.

I like to call this kind of understanding of signs the 'semiotic ladder'. According to this view, symbols are thought of as the highest rung, the pinnacle of semiotic competence. As an alternative view I propose the term 'semiotic matrix'. The idea of a matrix, in contrast to a uni-directional ladder, is suggestive of a multi-dimensional space. And the word 'matrix' is related to 'maternal': the semiotic matrix is the womb in which our representation and understanding of the world grows.

One of the mysteries of human evolution is the apparent delay between the emergence of symbolic language and the full flourishing of human culture and creativity. It's a fair bet that when the first anatomically modern humans appeared on the scene – people who were more or less indistinguishable physically from us – these people already had sophisticated symbolic spoken languages. The most obvious reason for drawing this conclusion is that they had anatomically modern voice boxes. The modern structure of the larynx must surely have evolved because it was selected for allowing the kind of rapid production of articulated sounds required by speech. And this means that the ancestors of these modern humans must have been using some kind of language; otherwise there would have been no 'selection pressure' for the evolution of even better ways of producing spoken sounds. If this seems odd it is worth noting that in human evolution the morphological changes associated with a particular behaviour tend to appear *after* the origin of the behaviour. For example, the discovery of how to use stone tools preceded, and was the cause of, the anatomical adaptations that favoured *efficient* tool use.

Anatomically modern humans appeared about 100,000 years ago. Therefore language dates at least that far back (probably much further). But the explosion of creative culture reflected, for example, in the beautiful cave art of the Upper Palaeolithic, did not appear until around 35,000 years ago. Why the delay? To some extent, the apparent delay may turn out to be partly an artefact of preservation. The Upper Palaeolithic 'revolution' was a European phenomenon, but evidence is beginning to turn up suggesting earlier cultural and artistic practices in Africa. I doubt, however, whether the vagaries of preservation are the entire explanation – I am with those who suspect there probably was a genuine delay between the emergence of fully symbolic articulate language and the cognitive revolution reflected in the famous horses of the Chauvet cave and the bulls of Lascaux.

So what was the cause of this delay? Well, the mystery would be resolved if the emergence of symbolic language was not the final step, the top rung of the process of human cognitive evolution. Suppose, instead, that there was another threshold to be crossed, namely the discovery of how to *combine* icons with symbols? That is to say, perhaps the final semiotic step that made modern humans what we are was entry into the 'semiotic matrix' – a whole new world of imagination and understanding opened up by learning the cognitive trick of juxtaposing or synthesizing different kinds of sign.

Suppose, for example, that one of our distant ancestors decided to keep track of the phases of the moon, night by night, by marking a notch for each night on a piece of antler bone. The sequence of notches would be indexically related to the succession of nights (since each notch would correspond directly to, and have been prompted by, the night in question).[8] But, as a whole, the sequence of notches is *iconically* related to the passage of time, perhaps over a month's cycle of phases of the moon. The artefact, originally made for some specific purpose, might now be the basis of the formation of an abstract concept such as 'time'. And whatever word (symbol) was introduced to label this concept, the concept would then acquire a life of its own within the semiotic repertoire of the individual and her community. Indeed, perhaps we humans could not conceive abstractly of 'time' until we had represented it (probably unintentionally) in an iconic form such as this.

My suggestion, then, is that human evolution may reflect the emergence of a capacity for using symbols, especially in the form

8 Alexander Marshack suggests such an origin for a pattern of notches he studied on a bone plaque found at the Blanchard rock shelter in the Dordogne: *The Roots of Civilization: The Cognitive Beginnings of Man's First Art, Symbol and Notation* (New York: Moyer Bell, 1991), pp. 43-48.

of spoken language, followed by the discovery of the power of combining different sign-types. Even this, I suspect, may be an oversimplification. Perhaps iconic elements – alongside symbolic ones – would have been a part of human thinking at an earlier stage than the above account would suggest. In that case, there might have been successive rounds of interplay between increasingly abstract iconic representations and increasingly sophisticated symbolic manipulations. On this slightly more refined version of the 'semiotic matrix' view, the delay between the appearance of articulate speech and the Upper Palaeolithic revolution may reflect the time taken for one or more iterations of this process.

So, semiotics may offer a currently under-explored way of asking questions about how humans evolved – a perspective that might draw scientific research away from the usual lampposts where the light is normally regarded as best. Exactly how these ideas about human evolution should be tested scientifically remains to be seen.[9] But do they mean anything theologically? One implication would be that what makes human cognition distinctive compared to other animals is a form of sign use that mirrors especially strongly the perichoretic (dance-like) interplay of the elemental grounds that I have been suggesting as a way of understanding the 'inner' life of the Trinity. This would not amount to an absolute difference between humans and other creatures, for such a dance of sign-types is no doubt played out to some degree in the kind of semiotic history of evolution that I touched on in the first part of this chapter. We might say, nevertheless, that human sign-use mirrors the *perichoresis* of the divine life especially clearly.

A related theological consequence of this understanding of human distinctiveness comes back to a point I made in Chapter 1, when we first met the technical meaning of the term 'symbol'. There I suggested that there is a 'folk' understanding of the meaning of 'symbol' that attributes to symbols a certain magical power. I expressed a concern that there is a tendency for theology (and other academic disciplines) to adopt a rather similar view, to the effect that symbols have some kind of privileged connection with the transcendent. This would fit well with what I have called the 'semiotic ladder' understanding of human evolution. Combining the two, we might come to think that humans have evolved the 'highest' form of semiotic capability, namely symbol use, and that this gives us special access, from the top rung of the semiotic ladder, to knowledge of God.

9 I am grateful to Terrence Deacon and Agustin Fuentes for ongoing discussions of these questions.

Understanding human distinctiveness as entry into a 'semiotic matrix' gives rise to a rather different view. On the perichoretic account, the dance of signs doesn't take us any 'higher'. There is no magical kind of sign that allows us to be lifted up and away from the ordinariness of the world into a more elevated realm. Rather, as the dance hots up, the world begins to become more 'transparent'. The interplay of sign-types begins to make the world into a 'window', not a 'ladder'.

The key difference between these two views is that the signs that begin to enable the world to become transparent to the transcendent are not special signs with magical powers, but ordinary signs with everyday effects. Think, for example, about how the 'ordinary' acts of baptism and Eucharist are able to actualize the Kingdom of God. This perspective, I think, requires a rather different understanding – compared to the 'magic symbol' view – of how God's grace works through the ordinary things and events of the world.

12

What God is Not

I have already alluded to the fact that the idea of vestiges of the Trinity in creation is currently regarded with a degree of suspicion, even hostility, within theological circles. The reasons for this are often traced back to the work of the great Swiss theologian Karl Barth (1886-1968). Barth's influential objections to the idea of vestiges of the Trinity stemmed from his misgivings about how such ideas can be used. In particular, Barth was concerned about the way in which, in Nazi Germany, Christianity's commitment to the primacy of revelation in Christ had been replaced by a liberal confidence in the power of human reason and in a 'natural theology'. The God of Jesus, a Jew executed for proclaiming salvation for all, had thereby become contorted into a god who underwrote the pursuit of absolute power and sanctioned the elimination of the Jewish people. The idea of vestiges of the Trinity in creation appeared dangerous to Barth because, used without due theological caution, it might offer leverage to such perversions of the Christian message. If we think we have it in our power to know about God by reflection on the created order rather than by submitting to God's gracious self-revelation, we will be constantly tempted to fashion an idea of God that suits our own sinful motives rather than being truly shaped by God's Christ-like love.

One way of rescuing the vestiges idea from Barth's criticisms would be to show how his concerns, while entirely justified, were appropriate to a particular historical context and need not be considered binding on religious reflection undertaken in other settings and with different motivations. Here, however, I am going to take a less direct and somewhat more positive route. Positive, that is, if sketching three things that God 'is not' can be said to be a positive exercise. My reason for attempting to deflect Barthian-style objections in this way is that I believe my approach to be vulnerable to such criticisms only if certain (false) assumptions about my position are read into what I am saying.

※

The first thing we should recognize is that God is not 'up there' or 'out there'. Neither, come to that, is God 'in here' or, indeed, anywhere.

It is often said that no one nowadays believes that God is an old man in the sky. I suspect, though, that this is only half true. Very few people believe that God is literally an old man. But many people (and I include myself in unguarded moments) tend to think of God being in some sense 'up there' or 'out there'. Of course, if asked about what is actually above the clouds, beyond the solar system, and so on, we will mostly be able to give some kind of scientifically informed answer. Such an answer is unlikely to support a cosmology in which God might be found somewhere among the planets or galaxies. But our prejudice remains, I think, that God resides somewhere 'up there' or 'out there'. If we try to correct this tendency by telling ourselves that God is equally 'in here', we are simply making the same mistake in a different way.

A minister recently illustrated the embodied nature of prayer by asking us in the congregation to fill balloons with successive puffs of air at key points during the intercessions. We were then invited to let go of the balloons so that our prayers might be released to God. To my mind the illustration was helpful. But it was interesting that, as far as I could see, we all released our balloons upwards. The balloons of course refused to follow a direct upward path: they spluttered and spiralled every which way, including over our heads and under our chairs. The balloons understood better than we did the difficulty in speaking about God's location.

Contemplating the fact that God is not anywhere requires a great effort, perhaps an impossibly great one given how used we are to ordinary objects being somewhere. But, if we make this effort, if we remind ourselves that God is not 'up there' (or in here, or anywhere), we will be protected to some degree from mistaking God for just one more (albeit very big and powerful) thing in the world. We can relate this to the diagram on p. 119, where the left-hand side of the diagram referred to God's triune being and the right-hand side referred to the vestiges of this tri-unity in the world. The principle that God is not another object somewhere in or outside the world amounts to saying that the division between the left and right sides of the diagram is not a difference between two essentially equivalent domains. Rather, the left–right divide in the diagram signifies the absolute otherness of God from the world. The arrows between God and the world therefore do not signify the operation of ordinary causal processes. Rather, they stand for the way in which God's creative work – and it is different in this regard from human creative activity – is the very *ground* of all creaturely existence, not merely its 'cause'.

It follows that the doctrine of the Trinity is not a theory about God in the same way that we have theories about things in the world. Ironically, one of the things that has helped to make the Trinity almost irrelevant to ordinary Christian faith and practice is a tendency to give trinitarian thinking too high a place in our theology. Or, rather, to give it the wrong sort of place. The problem arises if we take affirmation of the Trinity to be the zenith and goal of Christian understanding. That way of thinking might lead us to suppose that Christian discipleship should be directed towards achieving such an understanding and then pursuing its practical consequences. On this view, the doctrine of the Trinity is a theory about God and the task of Christians is continually to improve this theory; that is, to gain an ever more accurate understanding of God's inner being. But Christian discipleship is about learning how to follow Christ, not how to theorize about God. The 'semiotic model' of the Trinity is not an attempt to turn Christianity into an abstract philosophical system or an intellectual route to enlightenment. Instead, I offer it in the hope that, by seeing traditional theological claims from a new vantage point, we will find the paths of Christian discipleship easier to discern (though not necessarily easier to follow).

In short, if we remember that God is not out there, in here, or anywhere, then it will be easier to ensure that the pursuit of philosophy serves the calling of Christian discipleship rather than letting Christian discipleship become the servant of any philosophical scheme.

❀

The second thing we need to remember is that God is not a great cosmic designer or engineer.

This, again, runs counter to a fairly deep rooted assumption in much contemporary Christian thought. We are inclined to think about God as the all-powerful and supremely ingenious mind behind every detail of Nature's contrivances. The idea of God as a designer is typified by William Paley's notion of a divine 'watchmaker'. But if God can rightly be understood as an almighty engineer, it will be possible to deduce something about God's intentions and purposes from the empirical study of nature. From there one should be able to make inferences about the character and priorities of the Creator. This would indeed play into Barth's worst fears about 'natural theology' (including the notion of vestiges of the Trinity) for it would apparently invite a purely human exercise of investigating God's inner being.

Darwin's alternative hypothesis, that biological 'design' arises through evolution by natural selection rather than by divine fiat, is generally said to have dealt a fatal blow to the idea of God as a cosmic engineer. This was not, however, as devastating for traditional Christian thought as is often supposed. Historians point out that the idea that God's creative work is analogous to design or engineering is actually a rather recent one. The notion of God as primarily a designer arose in the late seventeenth and eighteenth centuries, when the mechanistic worldview deriving from Isaac Newton's discoveries was applied to religious thought. The outcome was, of course, shaped by a prevailing context of Enlightenment attitudes that were especially critical of 'revealed' theology and of the church. In other words the idea of God as designer or engineer is more an historical accident than a necessary part of a Christian doctrine of creation, and I want to emphasize that my account of the vestiges concept has nothing to do with it.

I am making no claim that God's imprinting of the possibilities of Quality, Otherness and Mediation into the structure of the world gives us any direct access to understanding God's character. As I have already made clear, although I think that God imprints and continually sustains this triadic structure within the world, God does not determine the content with which the world fills this structure. The freedom given to the created order is a reflection of its absolute otherness from God. The threefold structure imprinted on the world is more analogous to a canvas stretched across a frame, ready to be primed and painted upon, than to a design-engineer's detailed blueprint. The relation between the detailed features of the world and God's ultimate purposes is therefore less direct than the engineering analogy would imply. The possible presence of vestiges of the Trinity in creation does not, in itself, give us access to an understanding of these purposes. God's character, Christians affirm, has been fully and perfectly revealed in the person of Jesus. It is not belief in, or any model of, the Trinity that discloses this character; rather, the doctrine of the Trinity is an attempt to say what must be true of God *if it is the case* that God's Word has been fully and perfectly embodied within the fabric of the world.

Of course, if God is not properly thought of as a designer, the traditional 'argument from design' is no longer viable. If there is no 'design' in nature then we cannot infer the existence of a source of the design. This does not mean that we need rule out some kind of theistic argument based on the patterns of nature that I have been exploring in this book. However, such an argument would be more akin to what philosophers and theologians call a 'cosmological' argument than to a design argument.

One of the traditional cosmological arguments starts from the question, why is there something rather than nothing? The argument proposes that God, who brings things out of nothingness, is the best explanation of there being anything at all. In the context of my account of vestiges of the Trinity, this standard cosmological argument can be seen to correspond to the specific creative work of the Word. It is the Word who is the ground of the world's otherness from God, and hence the 'explanation' of how it is possible for any kind of world at all to exist. Note that this argument is entirely neutral with respect to what kind of world exists: the starting point is the existence of anything at all.

In the light of the semiotic model, this kind of cosmological argument can then be extended. As well as asking why there is any 'otherness' within the world and between the world and God, we can also ask why there is any 'quality' in the world. Note again that this is not a question about the origin of specific instances of beauty; rather, it is a question about why there is any beauty (or indeed any ugliness) at all. The trinitarian answer to this 'aesthetic' version of the cosmological question would be that it is the Father who is the ground of the possibility of all qualities within the world.

Finally, we can ask why there is any 'mediation' in the world. Why are there signs rather than no signs, intelligibility rather than unqualified meaninglessness, purpose rather than pure chaos? Einstein is said to have remarked that the most incomprehensible thing about the universe is that it is comprehensible. The trinitarian answer to this cosmological question of intelligibility is that such intelligibility points to the work of the Spirit. The Spirit is the ground of the possibility of all mediation in the world including the kinds of mediation involved in representation and interpretation, these being necessary if the world is to be in any way intelligible.

What I am saying, then, is that the semiotic model and my associated conjectures about vestiges of the Trinity in creation have no connection with the standard arguments from design or the kinds of natural theology with which those tend to be associated. That the world is structured by the kaleidoscopic patterns of Quality, Otherness and Mediation does, however, invite cosmological questions about the origins of these elemental grounds. The kinds of answer that might be given turn out to have an essentially trinitarian form.

Another way of putting this would be to say that the semiotic model is not an attempt to say something about what God is like on the basis of empirical observation of nature. Rather, it is an attempt to give a theological account of how it is that we can say anything at all about God. If God is absolutely other than the created order, how can anything about God be known? The answer suggested by the semiotic model is that creatures can know something of God because there is a consonance between the fundamental structure of the created order and the eternal being of God. Moreover, in the eternal being of God, *being* is identical with *signification*. Those two factors – the equivalence of being and knowing within God and the presence of likenesses or vestiges of this pattern within the created order – are what enable us to be able to say anything at all about God.

❀

The third thing to be recognized is that God is not the guarantor or underwriter of the present order of things.

This may seem a strange thing to say, given the emphasis I have placed on God's continual sustaining of the structure of the created order through the patterns of Quality, Otherness and Mediation. But it does not mean that God is necessarily happy with the precise way that the present world is structured or organized. Or, to put it another way, the primary task for the Christian is not unquestioningly to defend the present order of things but to discern what is, and what is not, a part of God's good purposes for creation.

Let me explain what I mean by saying something briefly about the problem of suffering and evil. In a nutshell, the problem is why a good, all-powerful God would allow suffering to occur. If God does not have the power to do whatever he wishes, is he really God? And if God does have such power but does not use it to prevent suffering, is he really good?

Very broadly speaking, attempts to answer these questions seem to fall into two main categories. On the one hand we have a set of responses that go by the name of 'theodicies'. These are attempts to justify God's actions (or inactions). One can argue, for example, that God's aim in creating the world was a certain kind of 'good', such as the emergence of free rational creatures capable of entering into genuine relationship with their Creator. The argument would then go on to say, for example, that such a goal can only be achieved if creation is given the kind of freedom in which suffering is a possibility. Obviously, there are many ways of developing arguments of this basic type. What they share is some kind of rational or logical defence of the way that God has decided what sort of world to create and sustain, when to act and when not to.

At the other end of the spectrum we find arguments to the effect that it is simply a mistake to attempt to justify God in this way. Conventional theodicies, it is said, are offensive to the victims of suffering (who do not want logical arguments about why God would have allowed such things to happen) and misunderstand God (failing to recognize the absolute otherness of God from creation and the utter inscrutability of God's purposes). I confess that I am instinctively attracted to this kind of anti-theodicy approach, partly because the standard theodicies often seem so thin in the face of actual suffering. But I also find myself ultimately dissatisfied with the anti-theodicy argument. For it seems to me that Christians need to be able to say *something* about God as Creator. It is not clear what room the anti-theodicists leave for this, because if God's purposes are so inscrutable as to defy rational discussion, where would one start if one wishes to speak about creation as God's work?

One of the points that is often made about the standard theodicies is that they have largely flourished in the period around and since the Enlightenment. Furthermore, they tend to treat God in a rather abstract philosophical way that can be, and often is, quite detached from any specifically Christian conception of God's character. But the rather philosophical tenor of the theodicist's work is not its only peculiarity, and the Enlightenment is not the only historical juncture that has influenced the nature of the exercise. It has been suggested that all theodicies are, in a sense, connected with a desire to defend the present order of things. Stanley Hauerwas has argued that this impulse only arose for Christians once Christianity became the state religion in the fourth century.[1] Before that, Christianity had no stake in defending the status quo; after it, Christians had good reason to think that maintaining more or less the present political and social order must be part of God's intentions for creation.

Obviously there would be a tangle of philosophical and historical complexity to be considered if one wished to defend this particular hypothesis in detail, and it may not be true of every form of theodicy. Nevertheless, I think it ought to point us in the direction of a useful

---

1 Stanley Hauerwas, *Naming the Silences: God, Medicine, and the Problem of Suffering* (Edinburgh: T. & T. Clark, 1993), pp. 55-58.

principle of reasoning for Christians. This principle would be as follows: we should not say anything about how God has made things in the beginning that is not informed by what we know of God's self-revelation in Jesus and by the kind of participation in God's life that this self-revelation invites.

If we submit to this principle, we will be alerted to the danger of looking at the present order of things and assuming that this is more or less how God intended things to be. This holds for the present social and political order. Perhaps it might even hold for what we can discern of the basic, apparently law-governed operation of the universe. After all, the exercise of looking for evidence of some kind of fine-tuning of the laws and constants of the universe and arguing that these may be exactly as they are in order to produce a particular kind of outcome is not, in the end, a particularly Christian approach to God's creative work (which is not to say that it is completely without value). Scripture does not say that God designed the laws of nature to guarantee the emergence of, say, free rational beings capable of loving their maker. Rather, we read that God "has made known to us his secret purpose, in accordance with the plan which he determined beforehand in Christ, to be put into effect when the time was ripe: namely, that the universe, everything in heaven and on earth, might be brought into a unity in Christ" (Ephesians 1: 9-10; Revised English Bible).

It has been said that we should say nothing about theodicy that could not be said in the presence of victims of horrendous suffering. The additional principle that I am advocating (and I do not claim any originality in doing so) is that we should say nothing about creation that cannot be said from the perspective of eschatology; from the perspective, that is, of the Kingdom announced and inaugurated by Jesus. Note that I am not suggesting that it is an error to regard Christian thinking about creation as having something to do with what God did "in the beginning." I cannot see what it would mean to say, as some theologians seem to, that God creates entirely "from the future." Creation, as I understand it, has aspects relating to past action, present sustaining and future promise. Where I think we make a mistake, though, is if we confuse Christian speech about creation with abstract speculation about how the present order of things may underpin God's ultimate purposes.[2] The Christian claim is that the world's past and present existence, and its future

2 I do not count my own scheme as 'abstract' in that sense because it derives ultimately from the question of how God's very quality of being can have become incarnate in the person of Jesus.

fulfilment, depends absolutely on God. I am not denying that there is an objective truth about what God 'did' at the 'beginning' of his creative work, or saying that we cannot in principle come to know something about this. However, I think we read God's purposes directly from the present order of things at our peril.

To put this another way, we should be continually questioning whether the present order of things is consistent with God's character and intentions, as revealed in the person of Jesus, and working to ameliorate or change that order where this seems desirable and possible. The relevance of the proposed principle for facing up to the theological aspects of the problem of suffering is that it allows us to hold on to both kinds of response mentioned above. On the one hand, it permits us to agree with those who are suspicious of the standard philosophical theodicies. Religious responses to suffering are not really searches for explanations of suffering in the abstract but attempts to make personal sense of actual suffering and to retain the hope of God's eventual triumph over evil.

On the other hand, we need not pursue this strategy so dogmatically that we pull the rug from under any attempt to speak of God's creative work "in the beginning." Rather, we are placing an epistemological constraint on Christian speech about creation, namely that whatever we say about creation must be said in the light of what we have learned about God through the life, death and resurrection of Jesus. Attempts to reason about why God has created a world in which suffering is possible are therefore not ruled out, especially where such accounts are strongly shaped by theological perspectives.[3] The proposed constraint would, however, ensure that we exercise great caution in inferring anything about God's purposes directly from the present structure of the world. The way things are – even if we cannot currently imagine that they could be any other way – can only legitimately be taken to reflect God's intentions for creation if such an inference makes sense in the light of what we believe to have been revealed about God's character and his promises for the future.

Obviously, it would be foolish to suggest that these brief remarks about theodicy amount to any significant contribution to the debate about the problem of evil. Certainly it is not my intention to let God 'off the hook' – that is, to side-step the troubling problem of why

---

3 See, for example, Christopher Southgate's groundbreaking work on suffering in evolution in *The Groaning of Creation: God, Evolution and the Problem of Evil* (Louisville, Kentucky and London: Westminster John Knox Press, 2008).

God has created a world in which suffering is even possible. In any case, I am less sure about what I have said in the last few paragraphs than about virtually anything else in the book. But the general approach I am advocating ought to suggest that my account of the 'vestiges' is not intended to replace God's self-revelation through the Word with a philosophical scheme that could easily be hijacked by an un-Christian social or political agenda. Crucially, nothing I've said about the elemental grounds of signification, or about the semiotic basis of our participation in God's life, is at variance with the principle that we should refrain from saying anything about creation that does not make sense in the light of the future revealed by the Word made flesh. For my whole argument is an attempt to make sense of the structure of the created order in the light of the Christian claim that, in the person of Jesus, the quality of God's very being has been fully and perfectly revealed. Such reflection leads me to conclude (and to rejoice) that God's sustaining of the world by the continual imprinting upon it of God's own eternal pattern of Quality, Otherness and Mediation is what enables us creatures, by our interpretative responses to the Word, to participate in God's very own life.

If we remember that God is not to be understood as the guarantor or underwriter of the present order of things, and if we discipline ourselves to avoid thinking that God is 'up there' (or 'in here') or is some kind of almighty engineer, then we will be able, I think, to speak of vestiges of the Trinity in creation without risking the kind of error that Barth was rightly so concerned to avoid.

13
Distinct but Inseparable

In Chapter 10 I invited you to see the three-ness of the world as a pattern of vestiges of the Trinity in creation. In doing so, I suggested that the Father may be understood as the creative ground of every worldly manifestation of Quality, the Word as the creative ground of every instance of Otherness, and the Spirit as the creative ground of every kind of Mediation.

Theologians have sometimes asked me to specify more precisely what I mean by 'creative ground'. What do I mean, for example, when I say that the Word is the creative ground of Otherness? In some ways, this is a question I have felt it reasonable to decline to answer. For, as I suggested at the end of Chapter 9, the relation between the created order and the uncreated Creator is something that can properly be called a mystery. Creator and creation are absolutely distinct, the gulf between the two is the ultimate kind of Otherness, and how the two relate or interact cannot be directly grasped by finite creatures.

Having said that, however, I do find myself prepared to try to say a little bit more on the subject. My justification for attempting to do so is that I will, in effect, be trying to articulate something that the tradition has long held to be true, that the creative activities of the three persons of the Trinity should be understood to be distinct but inseparable.

I should warn the reader that although this final chapter is very short, the going may get rather heavy. Anyone who does not find these further reflections helpful should therefore have no qualms about skipping to the summary of the book, which is followed by some ideas for meditations on the elemental grounds and their origins.

❧

I have already hinted that I am inclined to see the three elemental grounds – Quality, Otherness and Mediation – as underpinning not just the structure of signs but also the whole fabric of reality. One aspect of such a general underpinning of reality may begin to suggest itself if we ask ourselves how the three elements may be understood to relate to a triad already familiar to philosophers, namely possibility, actuality and generality.

Let me explain what I'm getting at, starting with 'actuality'. Actuality means what actually is. It is different from what isn't. In that sense there is a bruteness about actuality: it is there. Actuality is therefore an aspect or a manifestation of the element of Otherness. What is actual is Other than what isn't. And what is actual can directly impinge on us – its otherness can have actual effects.

What is actual was necessarily once possible (assuming that nothing impossible can ever be actual – for that is the definition of impossible). Possibilities are much more fleeting and evanescent than actualities. Possibilities share this characteristic of elusiveness with the element of Quality. Qualities are slippery, difficult to pin down. Of course we can't experience a quality unless it is actualized in some way. Even a quality that exists only in our imagination is actual: it is actualized in our mind. But whether imagined or concretely embodied, qualities – in themselves – are always threatening (or promising) to slip their moorings. Possibility and Quality are sisters in this respect, even twins.

This is where words fail, of course. As we noted earlier, the attempt to name the elemental grounds is a necessary convenience that ultimately can only point tentatively towards a deeper reality. As we saw at the end of Chapter 2, to name the elemental grounds is immediately to disturb them by introducing one or more of the other elements.

Anyway, what I am suggesting is that Otherness correlates with actuality and Quality correlates with possibility. At risk of being accused of shoehorning everything into a predetermined scheme (which not infrequently I am), Mediation then correlates with generality. A 'general', in the philosophical sense, is something that several things have in common. Four apples, four pears and four oranges have 'four-ness' in common. Three healthy individuals have 'health' in common. 'Four-ness' and 'health' are generals.

Whether generals are 'real' is a perennial philosophical question. Is 'health' something that exists in its own right, a 'thing' of some kind which our three individuals come to possess? Or is 'health' just a convenient way of pointing to something that only exists individually, something that is only real insofar as it is a convenient name for something we want to say about Janet, and separately about Jill, and separately again about John?

I side with those who are realists about generals. One of the reasons is that I believe that generals can be causally effective. For example, Janet may take up swimming, Jill cycling and John running, all because they want to pursue the general goal of 'health'. The same applies, for example, to the various ways in which general concepts such as justice and liberty may prompt us to act. The reality of generals also leads me to believe in the reality of evil, for it is possible for generals that are contrary to God's purposes to arise and to be causally effective in the world. That is the significance of the emphasis in the baptism service on committing ourselves to fight against evil. As I suggested in Chapter 7, the whole point of the sacrament of baptism is for us to renew and reform our understanding of the kinds of purpose (purposes being general goals) that rightly reflect a Spirit-guided response to the Word. When we reflect on the purposes and priorities of the church, we are prompted to actualize causally effective generals through which God's transformative grace can be active in the world.

Generality, then, is the mode of reality according to which distinct things can have something in common. Generals (of which health, justice and liberty are examples) connect things together – they mediate between things. Hence, generality is a manifestation of the element of Mediation.

❀

To summarize: Otherness correlates with actuality, Quality correlates with possibility and Mediation correlates with generality. In other words, the elemental grounds whose interactions and ramifications we have been pursuing in this book turn out to have correspondences with the metaphysical triad of possibility, actuality and generality.

Now look again at part of the diagram we met previously in Chapter 10 (p. 119). This is the part that relates specifically to the idea of vestiges of the Trinity in creation:

Notice that in this part of the diagram I have drawn the lines between the trinitarian persons and the corresponding elemental grounds not as parallel but as crossing one another. This is intended to convey the idea of some kind of co-operation between Father, Son/Word and Spirit in their creative activities.

Consider, for example, the relation between the Word (the square on the left) and Otherness in the world (the square on the right).

The primary relation between the two is represented by the arrow between them. According to my way of thinking about this relation (developed in Chapter 10) we can say that the Word is the *creative ground* of all otherness in the world.

For the Word to be the *ground* of Otherness in the world the Word itself must *be* the relation of Otherness. But with the triad of possibility, actuality and generality in mind, we can elaborate a little on that way of putting it. We may now see that for instances of otherness in the world to be real, three further things are required.

First, otherness within the world must be made *possible*. We have seen that possibility correlates with the elemental ground of Quality. Making worldly instances of otherness *possible* is therefore the work of the Father (even though their primary creative ground is the Son/ Word).

Second, instances of otherness within the world must be permitted to become *actual*. We have seen that actuality correlates with the elemental ground of Otherness. Making worldly instances of otherness *actual* is therefore the work of the Son/Word (in addition to, or rather as part of, the Son/Word's role as the primary creative ground of Otherness).

Third, all instances of otherness must share something in common, namely 'otherness'. In other words, the many different kinds of otherness must have a generality about them. We have seen that generality correlates with the elemental ground of Mediation. The work of the Spirit allows different kinds of otherness to have Otherness in common (again, working in conjunction with the Son/ Word, through whom Otherness is primarily grounded).

If we were fully to express the relation between God's otherness (the otherness of Father from Son) and instances of otherness in the world we would say that:

> The Word is the creative ground of the *possibility* of the *actualization* of individual instances of the *general* form of Otherness in the world.

The italicized words are the ones corresponding to the distinct but inseparable work of the Father, Son and Spirit respectively.

In a shortened form we might say that the Word is the creative ground of the possibility of all Otherness. Or, simply, as we did originally, that the Word is the creative ground of Otherness.

Behind the simpler forms, however, would lie the recognition that each person of the Trinity is necessarily involved in this relation of grounding. This is what is rather inadequately expressed by making the arrows in the vestiges part of the diagram cross over one another. It is a visual representation of the fact that each of the three distinct grounding relations (Otherness grounded in the Word, Quality grounded in the Father, Mediation grounded in the Spirit) operates only by virtue of the co-operation of the other persons of the Trinity.

I shall leave it to the reader, if they wish, to complete the account by formulating the full expressions of the grounding relations between the Father (the circle on the left) and instances of Quality in the world (the circle on the right), and between the Spirit (the triangle on the left) and instances of Mediation in the world (the triangle on the right). The pattern of these formulae will of course be the same as that of the long form of the formula above relating the eternal Word to instances of Otherness in the world. And, in each case, the formula will be a way of expressing the distinct but inseparable creative activities of the Father, Son and Holy Spirit.

Summary

In this book I have set out three main ideas. The first is that what we know of the structure of signs may offer the basis of a 'semiotic model' of the Trinity. The second is that the semiotic model leads to a way of understanding how creatures may be able to participate in God's own life. The third is that the structure of signs – and perhaps the very structure of existence – is a reflection of the mode of God's continual creative activity. In other words, it is possible to discern patterns within the world that may be understood as vestiges of the Trinity in creation.

The following paragraphs offer a summary of the arguments I have presented. The order differs from that of the order of the chapters. This is simply because the sequence in which I have felt it would be most helpful for the reader to be introduced to the ideas is not necessarily the order in which they are most usefully summarized. More fundamentally, it reflects the fact that the book does not consist of one long deductive argument, but an attempt to present a new way of looking at the way in which Christian theology and Christian life may hold together. For that reason any of the individual elements of the argument could, in principle, provide the entry point to the whole.

My proposal, then, may be summarized as follows.

1. We live and move and have our being in a world of signs. We are surrounded by naturally occurring signs and by signs that have been produced for the purpose of signifying. We are compulsive makers and interpreters of signs. Compulsive not simply because we happen to be good at it, but because our capacity for representation and interpretation is what has shaped us as a species and forms us as persons.

2. Although the variety of signs is endless, all signs have the same basic underlying structure. A sign is something that stands for something else. An interpretation is a purposeful response to a sign, where the sign mediates between the object and the interpreter. Interpretations are fallible: they can be mistaken. But signs nevertheless have a capacity to connect with reality.

3. The triad of sign, object and interpretation can be dissected into a further series of triads. The sign–object relation can be iconic, indexical or symbolic. The sign-in-itself can be a quali-sign, stand-alone sign or rule-produced sign. An interpretation can be a feeling, an action or a thought.

4. When the relationships of sign, sign–object relation and interpretation are considered in the most general terms, they can be understood as manifestations of three elemental grounds of signification: Quality, Otherness and Mediation. Furthermore, when the triadic sub-divisions of these relations are examined they are found, likewise, to be characterized by these three elemental grounds. In other words, Quality, Otherness and Mediation underpin and ramify through the structure of signs at every level and in every dimension.

5. The elemental grounds have striking resonances with traditional Christian affirmations about the three persons of the Trinity. Quality recalls the unoriginate-ness (unbegotten-ness) of the Father. Otherness correlates with the distinction of the Son from the Father. Mediation corresponds with the mediatory action of the Spirit, the bond between Father and Son. These similarities offer the basis of a semiotic model of the Trinity.

6. The semiotic model of the Trinity suggests a way of understanding the mutual indwelling of the persons and their dynamic interactions. The 'kaleidoscopic' patterns of Quality, Otherness and Mediation, as they play out in the multi-dimensional processes of signification, offer a way of picturing the eternal perichoretic dance of the Father, Son and Spirit. In other words, *semiosis* models *perichoresis*.

7. The semiotic model offers to resolve some of the perennial tensions in Christian thinking about the Trinity. Like the psychological analogies it is able to affirm that the persons are distinct and yet bound together in an inseparable unity. In doing so, however, the model avoids any implication that the human mind is an isolated autonomous entity. Rather, like the social model of the Trinity, it affirms the social and relational basis of human being. It does so by pointing to the semiotic basis of human relationality, thus grounding human relationality in the being of God without implying a direct analogy between three humans and the tri-unity of God. Indeed, the semiotic model offers a new understanding of the nature of relations, according to which Quality, Otherness and Mediation are seen to be three distinct kinds of relation. God is therefore not made subject to a general concept of 'relation', but is the source of all relationality.

8. In the created order, the dance of signs is characteristic not only of humans, but can be traced through all living things back to the simplest organisms. Indeed, the origin of life may be understood as the first emergence of a capacity for interpretation of the environment. The increasing complexity of organisms through the processes of evolution is a reflection, in part, of increasingly complex and sophisticated capacities for sign-use and sign-interpretation.

9. Humans are especially sophisticated users of signs. Indeed, what makes humans distinct from other creatures is our capacity richly to combine and juxtapose different kinds of sign. This does not reflect ascent of a hierarchy of sign-types but entry into a semiotic matrix. In certain conditions this matrix is able to become transparent to the transcendent – not because of the existence of some special or magical kind of sign, but because of the God-given revelatory capacity of ordinary signs.

10. The three-ness of sign-processes in the world can be understood as either an analogy, a likeness or a vestige of the three-ness of God's eternal triune life. As an analogy, the three-ness of God would be understood as a projection from our knowledge of the world. As a likeness, the three-ness of the world would be understood as intentionally imparted by God. As a vestige, the three-ness of the world would be understood as not merely imparted but also imprinted by the creative activities of Father, Son and Spirit. The concept of vestiges of the Trinity in creation is often regarded with suspicion by theologians. However, it offers a more attractive and (in spite of current theological prejudices) a theologically more coherent understanding of the creative work of the Trinity than the alternatives. It also suggests a way of understanding how the activities of the Father, Son and Spirit are distinct but inseparable.

11. Jesus understood his life as an enacted parable of the triumphant return of YHWH to Jerusalem. As such, his ministry was shaped and framed by various signs, especially certain iconic signs of the arrival of the Kingdom. The Temple action and the Last Supper can be understood in this way. Jesus' life and death as a whole can be understood as an embodiment and enactment of the quality of God's presence. This view gives rise to a semiotic approach to understanding the Christian concept of the Incarnation. According to this view, Jesus, in his total life, ministry and death, embodied a quali-sign of the eternal nature of God.

12. The quali-sign understanding of the Incarnation has the potential to avoid the ever-present tendency to docetism in Christian thinking. That is, it avoids the view that Jesus was somehow God in a human disguise, that he was not entirely and fully human. Similarly, the semiotic approach to the Incarnation affirms a non-dualistic view of human being, in which there is no part of the human person (mind, soul, etc.) that can be removed and replaced with a divine part. The idea that the totality of a person's life and death can be a quali-sign also suggests a possible view of resurrection according to which the resurrection body would be understood as the quality of the person's whole life held eternally in God's presence.

13. The life of the Trinity is the Spirit's eternal interpretation of the Word as the perfect representation of the Father. The neglected heart of the structure of Christian faith is the claim that we are called to become 'partakers' of this divine nature. We participate in the divine life when we rightly interpret the Word as the perfect sign of the Father. In that case, we are being adopted into the place of the Spirit in the Trinity, who is the eternal interpreter of the Word. This is not merely a matter of intellectual knowledge. The fullness of our being is engaged in this interpretative work when our response to the Word involves our feelings and actions as well as our thoughts.

14. Any interpretation involves a change in the interpreter. It follows that when the Spirit eternally interprets the Word, the Spirit is 'changed'. Since any change in the eternal Trinity cannot result in any imperfection in God, this change in the Spirit cannot become a sign of anything less than the perfect goodness of the Father. In other words, the eternal dynamic of the Trinity can only ever generate further signs of the Father, i.e., further expressions of the Word. Therefore, when we are adopted into the place of the Spirit within the Trinity, we are similarly transformed into a likeness of the Word. And in being so transformed into the likeness of Christ, we are adopted into the place of the Word within the eternal life of God.

15. A sacrament is a sign that actualizes what it signifies, where what is actualized is the Kingdom of God. The Eucharist is a sacrament that involves a collective response to the Word, modelled on Jesus' table fellowship with sinners and outcasts and thereby imaging the heavenly banquet that will be the fulfilment of the Kingdom. In this

response to Jesus' call we are adopted into the place of the Spirit and collectively transformed into the likeness of the Word, the body of Christ. The Eucharist is a template for those habits of feeling, thought and action which are the basis of the growth of God's Kingdom in the world.

16. When we rightly interpret something in the world as even partially imaging God, we draw that thing or person into the life of the Trinity by having them take the place of the Word's eternal representation of the Father. Because we are able intentionally to shape and nurture parts of the created order into better likenesses of God, we have a grace-dependent means of using our imaging, and interpretation of such imaging, as the basis of a runaway process, drawing one another into God's life. The sacrament of baptism is an example of, and model for, that process.

17. The scapegoating theory of atonement fits well with the semiotic model of the Trinity and the associated quali-sign understanding of the Incarnation. The quality of God's being that is specifically revealed in the person of Jesus is God's power of creating without victimization or sacrifice. The scapegoating mechanisms of exclusion and blame on which we normally rely for our personal and social peace are laid bare in Jesus' life and death. By completing the trajectory of the progressive recognition of this mechanism, narrated in the Hebrew Scriptures, Jesus finally undoes the mechanism and offers an alternative kind of peacemaking. The quali-sign approach to the Incarnation and the wider semiotic model of the Trinity show why this does not amount to a merely exemplarist Christology. Rather, the possibility of the embodiment of the very quality of God's being in creation is a fully objective reality, actualized in the person of Jesus. Jesus' resurrection and ascension are confirmation that this total quality of Jesus' life is the eternal Word, the full and perfect representation of the Father.

18. The church is holy, catholic and apostolic to the extent that it is transformative, truthful and inclusive. It is transformative (holy) when it is the locus of our interpretation of the Word as the perfect sign of the Father, thus drawing us, and with us the whole of creation, into the eternal life of God. It is truthful (catholic) to the extent that it makes its unity a product of its honest seeking after the truth, rather than seeking to guard some established view of the truth by efforts to maintain its unity. It is called to be inclusive (apostolic) in the sense that it must reject victimization and exclusion as its modes of constitution.

19. Recent ecumenical convergences in theological understanding of the Eucharist reflect these marks of the church in a way that the semiotic model supports. The semiotic approach makes sense of the real presence of Christ in the Eucharist as a transformation of the assembled church into the body of Christ. The recovery of the eschatological (future-oriented) and pneumatological (Spirit-inspired) dimensions of the Eucharist cohere with the non-foundationalist yet realist epistemology implied by a semiotic model. The quali-sign/scapegoating understanding of the Incarnation is consistent with recent ecumenically accepted insights into the 'sacrificial' character of the Eucharist.

20. A recurring theme in all of the above is that there is nothing magical or mysterious about the structure of signification as such, or about the kinds of sign involved in God's self-revelation to the world. The 'mystery' lies only in the fact, if true, that it is possible for the absolute divide between Creator and creation to be bridged. The semiotic model offers a philosophical and theological framework within which such an affirmation can make sense, without claiming to dissolve the mystery. The key ideas in this framework are 1. The eternal being of God is essentially representational: the Spirit eternally interprets the Word as the perfect sign of the Father. 2. The processes of representation and interpretation in the world are vestiges of the Trinity in creation in the strong sense of bearing the intentional direct imprint of the distinct but inseparable activities of the Father, Son and Spirit. 3. The structure of signs is a gift to the world, through which creatures may, by grace, become participants in the eternal triune life of God.

21. The claim that the world is structured according to a pattern that reflects the continual creative activity of Father, Son and Spirit gives rise to the possibility of what I call a spirituality of ordinary experience, a mysticism of the everyday. A set of meditations that explore such a spirituality follows below. This spirituality of ordinary experience is not itself the goal of the Christian life, but may help to keep that life grounded in a recognition of its source, namely, the Spirit's eternal interpretation of the Word as the perfect sign of the Father.

Meditations

The following 'exercises' are intended to offer a pattern for prayer or meditation that reflects and, I hope, reinforces the way of understanding the Trinity that I have offered in this book.

There are seven meditations so you may wish to spread them over a week, or repeat them over a cycle of several weeks. In that case, if you start the first exercise on a Wednesday, the exercise most closely related to resurrection will fall on Sunday. However, the timing of the exercises in relation to particular days of the week is not essential.

The meditations follow a perichoretic path from Quality, through Otherness, to Mediation, then back through Otherness to Quality, and then again via Otherness to Mediation. With a little practice you may find that you can call to mind a particular exercise in a few seconds in the middle of a busy day or as part of some other prayer or meditation.

I submit that there is no conceivable setting, situation or form of experience which could not be co-opted as raw material for these meditations. In that sense I like to think of them as the basis of a kind of mysticism of the everyday, a spirituality of the ordinary. They are able to be so, I believe, because there is nothing in creation that is not held in being by the continual creative activity of the Father, Son and Spirit.

In short, the meditations draw our attention to the omnipresence of the imprint of God's creative work; that is, to vestiges of the Trinity in creation.

Taste and see that the LORD is good.

Psalm 34: 8

God is love.

1 John 4: 8

Notice

A quality. (Anything that you can currently see/hear/taste/smell/touch.)

Reflect

On how every quality in the world witnesses to the possibility of quality and points to the ultimate quality – the quality of God's love.

Give thanks

For something beautiful or good.

He is the image of the invisible God . . .

Colossians 1: 15

Notice

A difference. (Two different colours, a boundary between two things, etc.)

Reflect

On how Otherness is fundamental to representation. It enables something to stand for something else.

Give thanks

That God represents (reveals) God's-self to the world.

Likewise the Spirit helps us in our weakness; for we do not know how to pray as we ought, but that very Spirit intercedes with sighs too deep for words.

Romans 8: 26

Notice

Something that connects (mediates between) two other things. (Minimally, a line or continuous colour, etc.)

Reflect

On how without the mediating work of the Spirit there would be nothing but action and reaction; noisy gongs and clanging cymbals.

Pray

That, as the ground of mediation and interpretation, the Spirit will come to give us wisdom, understanding and discernment.

In the beginning was the Word. . . . All things came into being through him, and without him not one thing came into being.

John 1: 1-3

Notice

The brute actuality of things; that everything is created from nothing.

Reflect

On how the world is utterly other than God, an otherness grounded in the Otherness of the Word from the Father.

Pray

That human creativity may seek to mirror God's creation 'out of nothing'; creation without using, excluding or victimizing others.

Philip said to him, 'Lord, show us the Father, and we will be satisfied.' Jesus said to him, 'Have I been with you all this time, Philip, and you still do not know me? Whoever has seen me has seen the Father.'

John 14: 8-9

Notice

The quality of being that is your own self, your own personality or 'soul'.

Reflect

On how the fabric of the world is such as to be able to embody the very quality of God.

Give thanks

For the promise of the 'resurrection of the body', the summation of our total quality of personal being.

And all of us, with unveiled faces, seeing the glory of the
Lord as though reflected in a mirror, are being transformed
into the same image from one degree of glory to another . . .

2 Corinthians 3: 18

Notice

Anything or anyone that/who reflects something of the glory
(quality) of God.

Reflect

On how, when we rightly interpret the Word (or anything else) as
an image of the Father so we are drawn into the very life of God and
transformed by that act of interpretation into a closer likeness of the
Word's glory.

Pray

That we may recognize Christ's likeness in all people.

Thus he has given us, through these things, his precious
and very great promises, so that through them you may
escape from the corruption that is in the world because of
lust, and may become participants in the divine nature.

2 Peter 1: 4

Notice

Your response to the news that God's promise is to make us
participants in the divine nature.

Reflect

On how participation in the divine nature happens here and now, in
our everyday interpretative responses to things and people, and in
the signs we ourselves make and become.

Pray

That the whole of creation may, through the freedom of the glory
of the children of God, be released from its groaning and come to
participate in the divine life.

Glossary

Economic Trinity. See immanent Trinity.

Elemental grounds (sometimes shortened to elements). My collective term for the most fundamental constituents of signification (and perhaps of reality). The three elemental grounds are Quality, Otherness and Mediation.

Epistemology. The philosophical study of how we know whatever we know. Ontology, in contrast, is concerned with what there is, rather than with how we know about what there is.

Immanent Trinity. The Father, Son and Spirit as they relate to one another within God's own eternal being. This is distinguished from (but should not be disconnected from) the economic Trinity, which is the Father, Son and Spirit as they are revealed, act and are experienced within the world.

Incarnation. The Christian claim that the very being of God became embodied in the person of Jesus of Nazareth.

Interpretation. A purposeful response to a sign made by an agent. The three kinds of interpretation are feelings, actions and thoughts.

Mediation. The elemental ground (see above) characterized by connection, continuity and generality.

Ontology. See epistemology.

Otherness. The elemental ground (see above) characterized by otherness/difference/actuality.

Perichoresis. The dynamic mutual indwelling of the Father, Son and Spirit.

Quality. The elemental ground (see above) characterized by 'in-itself-ness'; just being what it is, sheer possibility.

Sacrament. A sign that actualizes what it signifies where what is actualized is the Kingdom of God. The main sacraments discussed are baptism and the Eucharist.

Semiosis. A term used in the field of semiotics for the processes of representation and interpretation.

Semiotics. The philosophical field concerned with the study of signs, representations and interpretations.

Signification. A general term covering any process of representation or interpretation.

Sign-in-itself (sometimes referred to as simply the sign). Something that stands as a sign for something else. The three kinds of sign-in-itself are quali-signs, stand-alone signs and rule-produced signs.

Sign–object relation. The relationship between the sign and whatever the sign represents (stands for). The three kinds of sign–object relation are icon, index and symbol.

Theosis. The process of participation in, or union with, God's being or nature.

Trinity. God revealed as three 'persons' in one nature, the 'persons' of the Trinity being traditionally named as Father, Son (Word) and Spirit.

Vestiges of the Trinity in creation. In traditional thinking, the idea that creation bears certain likenesses to the triune being of God. In my account, the even stronger idea that creation bears the imprint of God's activity of creating through the Word and Spirit.

Select Bibliography

Alison, James. *Knowing Jesus*. London: SPCK, 2nd revised edition, 1998.

St Augustine. *The Trinity*. Translated by Edmund Hill, OP. New York: New City Press, 1991.

Crockett, William R. *Eucharist: Symbol of Transformation*. Collegeville, Minnesota: Liturgical Press, 1989.

Deacon, Terrence. *The Symbolic Species: The Co-evolution of Language and the Human Brain*. New York and London: W.W. Norton & Co, 1997.

Gunton, Colin E. *The Triune Creator: A Historical and Systematic Study*. Edinburgh: Edinburgh University Press, 1998.

Hoffmeyer, Jesper. *Signs of Meaning in the Universe*. Translated by Barbara J. Haveland. Bloomington and Indianapolis: Indiana University Press, 1996.

LaCugna, Catherine Mowry. *God For Us: The Trinity and Christian Life*. San Francisco: HarperSanFrancisco, 1991.

Robinson, Andrew. *God and the World of Signs: Trinity, Evolution and the Metaphysical Semiotics of C.S. Peirce*. Leiden: Brill, 2010.

Short, T.L. *Peirce's Theory of Signs*. Cambridge: Cambridge University Press, 2007.

Wright, N.T. *Jesus and the Victory of God*. London: SPCK, 1996.

Notes on bibliographic selection

The books listed above have been particularly significant to me at various phases of the development of my thinking and would offer good starting points for further reading. Chapter numbers referred to below are those in *Traces of the Trinity* (*TT*) to which these works most closely relate.

Catherine LaCugna traces the way in which the doctrine of the Trinity becomes irrelevant if it is separated from Christian life (*TT* Chapters 1 and 5). Her position probably leans more towards standard 'social trinitarianism' than mine.

T.L. Short's book is, in my opinion, the best available account of Peirce's semiotics (*TT* Chapters 1-4). Short's account differs from mine in that he does not accept that signs are operative in organisms simpler than higher animals (*TT* Chapter 11).

Augustine developed a theory of signs which is reflected in his understanding of the Trinity (*TT* Chapter 2). However, his idea of 'vestiges' of the Trinity is closer to my 'likenesses' than it is to my strong version of the vestiges concept (*TT* Chapter 10).

N.T. Wright's controversial thesis about Jesus' self-understanding suggested a way of thinking about the Incarnation in semiotic terms (*TT* Chapter 4). James Alison's short book offers an introduction to the scapegoating theory of atonement (*TT* Chapter 8).

William Crockett's outline of the history of eucharistic thought and practice influenced my thinking about the ecclesiological implications of my semiotic account of the sacraments (*TT* Chapter 9).

Colin Gunton's study led me to reflect on the idea that God creates through his two 'hands', the Word and Spirit, though Gunton would have resisted linking the trinitarian mediation of creation to the concept of vestiges of the Trinity (*TT* Chapter 10).

I first came to biosemiotics, and hence to Peirce, through reading Jesper Hoffmeyer's work. There is a growing literature on biosemiotics but I retain a particular affection for *Signs of Meaning in the Universe* (*TT* Chapter 11).

Terrence Deacon's book is a groundbreaking application of Peirce's semiotics to the field of human evolution, which my concept of the 'semiotic matrix' attempts to supplement (*TT* Chapter 11).

God and the World of Signs is my own proposal for a 'semiotic model' of the Trinity, which *Traces of the Trinity* aims to clarify and develop.

Index

BV - #0046 - 200521 - C0 - 234/156/9 - PB - 9780227174432 - Matt Lamination